Tax Processes for Businesses

(Finance Act 2023)

Workbook

for assessments from 29 January 2024

Jo Osborne

Published by Osborne Books Limited
Tel 01905 748071
Email books@osbornebooks.co.uk
Website www.osbornebooks.co.uk

Design by Laura Ingham

Printed by CPI Group (UK) Limited, Croydon, CR0 4YY, on environmentally friendly, acid-free paper from managed forests.

British Library Cataloguing in Publication Data
A catalogue record for this book is available from the British Library

ISBN 978-1-911681-04-5

Contents

Introduction

Chapter activities

Answers to chapter activities

Practice assessments

Answers to practice assessments

AAT Reference material

Introduction

Qualifications covered

This book has been written specifically to cover the Unit 'Tax Processes for Businesses' which is mandatory for the following qualifications:

- AAT Level 3 Diploma in Accounting
- AAT Level 3 Certificate in Bookkeeping
- AAT Diploma in Accounting – SCQF Level 7

This book contains Chapter Activities which provide extra practice material in addition to the activities included in the Osborne Books Tutorial text, and Practice Assessments to prepare the student for the computer based assessments. The latter are based directly on the structure, style and content of the sample assessment material provided by the AAT at www.aat.org.uk.

Suggested answers to the Chapter Activities and Practice Assessments are set out in this book.

Osborne Study and Revision Materials

Additional materials, tailored to the needs of students studying this unit and revising for the assessment, include:

- **Tutorials:** paperback books with practice activities
- **Student Zone:** access to Osborne Books online resources
- **Osborne Books App:** Osborne Books ebooks for mobiles and tablets

Visit www.osbornebooks.co.uk for details of study and revision resources and access to online material.

Chapter activities

1 Introduction to Value Added Tax

1.1 VAT paid by a customer on a purchase invoice is treated as which of the following in the supplier's VAT Return?

Select **one** option.

Income Tax	
Input tax	
Output tax	
Sales tax	

1.2 Decide whether the statement below is true or false.

'VAT is a direct tax.'

TRUE / FALSE

1.3 A sales invoice for taxable supplies that includes standard rate VAT is being processed by a VAT-registered business. What will be the effect of this invoice on the VAT due to be paid by this business to HMRC?

Select **one** option.

It will have no effect on the VAT payable by the business	
It will increase the amount of VAT due to be paid	
It will decrease the amount of VAT due to be paid	

1.4 A VAT-registered business issues a credit note to one of its customers. The credit note is for £100 plus VAT at 20%, and relates to an original invoice of £560 plus VAT at 20%. What will be the effect on the VAT due to be paid to HMRC?

Select **one** option.

It will increase the VAT payable by £20	
It will decrease the VAT payable by £20	
It will increase the VAT payable by £112	
It will decrease the VAT payable by £112	

1.5 A retailer buys goods from the manufacturer for £500 plus VAT of £100. It then sells them to a customer for £800 plus VAT of £160. How is the total VAT of £160 paid to HMRC?

Select **one** option.

All £160 is paid over to HMRC by the customer	
All £160 is paid over to HMRC by the retailer	
The retailer pays £60, and the manufacturer pays £100 to HMRC	
The manufacturer pays the whole £160 to HMRC	

1.6 An invoice that includes goods at reduced rate VAT means that the rate of VAT charged on these goods is which of the following?

Select **one** option.

0%	
5%	
17.5%	
20%	

1.7 Which of the following would be a reason for a business to choose to voluntarily deregister for VAT?

Select **one** option.

It only supplies standard-rated products	
Whilst it previously supplied standard-rated products, it now only supplies products that attract reduced rate VAT	
The owner of the business is winding the business down prior to retiring	
The business only supplies zero-rated products	

1.8 Which of the following businesses can **voluntarily** register for VAT?

Select **one** option.

A business that only supplies products which are exempt from VAT	
An individual who sells his/her own second-hand clothing on eBay	
A business that annually supplies standard-rated goods with a list price of £47,000	
A business that supplies exempt goods with a list price of £98,000	

1.9 A business that registers for VAT receives which of the following as proof that it has registered?

Select **one** option.

A VAT Return	
Certificate of registration	
Trading certificate	
VAT control account	

1.10 Fistrall Ltd submits its first VAT Return on 30 June 2023. Which of these is the last year that Fistrall Ltd must retain its business records relating to this VAT Return?

Select **one** option.

2025	
2027	
2029	
2030	

1.11 Jensters Ltd has failed to register for VAT, despite being aware that it should have done so on 30 April 2022.

What is the maximum penalty that the business could face for this?

Select **one** option.

20% of potential lost revenue	
50% of potential lost revenue	
70% of potential lost revenue	
100% of potential lost revenue	

1.12 Decide whether the following statement is true or false.

'Businesses are permitted to store their business records digitally.'

TRUE / FALSE

1.13 A business reached the VAT registration threshold three months ago but did not register for VAT. It is now required to pay HMRC £7,500 in respect of output tax that it did not charge during this three month period.

Decide whether the following statement is true or false.

'The business's customers must now reimburse the business for the output tax payable to HMRC.'

TRUE / FALSE

1.14 Anoosh starts trading on 1 April 2024. His taxable sales to the end of September are £47,220. In October Anoosh saw a significant increase in business, and turnover for that month was £42,080.

By what date must Anoosh register for VAT?

Select **one** option.

30 April 2024	
31 October 2024	
30 November 2024	
1 April 2025	

1.15 In September 2023 Ryder Ltd started trading, selling bicycles and cycle helmets, and business has been growing steadily. Bicycles are standard-rated for VAT, but cycle helmets are classified as zero-rated. Its sales for the first few months are shown in the table below.

	Bicycles £	Cycle helmets £
September 2023	9,400	2,500
October 2023	11,200	3,200
November 2023	15,700	4,450
December 2023	18,400	4,300
January 2024	19,000	4,800
February 2024	19,800	5,100
March 2024	20,000	5,300

At the end of which month will Ryder Ltd exceed the VAT threshold?

2 VAT and business documents

2.1 There are a number of items that must be included on a full VAT invoice.

From the list below tick all items that must be included on a full VAT invoice.

	Must be included on a full VAT invoice
Customer order number	
Invoice date	
Description of the goods or services supplied	
Customer's VAT number	
Seller's VAT number	
Customer's name and address	
Seller's name and address	
Seller's required payment method	
Rate of prompt payment discount (if offered)	
VAT rates applied	
Amount excluding VAT	
Amount of VAT charged	

2.2 Reynolds Ltd is registered for VAT and supplies some goods that are standard-rated for VAT and some goods on which VAT is charged at reduced rate. The invoice for one of its customers includes items at both these rates of VAT.

Which of the following statements about the VAT invoice that Reynolds Ltd issues to this customer is true?

Select **one** option.

The invoice should only show the total VAT charges	
The invoice should show the standard rate VAT and the reduced rate VAT as separate amounts on the invoice	
The invoice should show the standard rate VAT separately and include the reduced rate VAT in the Gross amount due	
The invoice should show the reduced rate VAT separately and include the standard rate VAT in the Gross amount due	

2.3 Complete the following sentence by inserting the correct figure.

'A business can issue a simplified invoice if the amount charged for the supply, including VAT, is

£[   ] or less.'

2.4 A business makes mixed supplies to a customer as follows:

- standard-rated supplies of £100 plus VAT of £20
- exempt supplies of £97

Decide which of the following statements is correct in this situation.

Select **one** option.

The business can issue a simplified invoice as the total supplies including VAT are less than £250	
The business can issue a simplified invoice as the total supplies excluding VAT are less than £250	
The business cannot issue a simplified invoice as the invoice includes exempt supplies	
Simplified invoices cannot be issued if there are mixed supplies	

2.5   Jason makes mixed supplies to a customer as follows:

- standard-rated supplies of £100 plus VAT of £20

- zero-rated supplies of £97

Which **one** of the following amounts **must** be included on the simplified invoice that Jason issues?

£20	
£97	
£100	
£120	
£217	

2.6   On 15 November, Design Hub Ltd issued an invoice to Vimal J Ltd for £3,240, including standard rate VAT. Vimal J Ltd paid 60% of the invoice on 22 November and then paid the remaining 40% on 20 December.

(a)   What is the actual tax point for this transaction?

Select **one** option.

15 November	
22 November	
30 November	
20 December	

(b)   How much output tax, relating to this transaction, should be included in the VAT Return for the quarter ended 30 November?

£ [   ]

2.7 Which of the following statements are true about a pro-forma invoice?

Identify **all** statements that are true.

	True about a pro-forma invoice
Pro-forma invoices must show the supplier's VAT registration number	
Pro-forma invoices are normally used to collect payment from a customer prior to supplying the goods	
Pro-forma invoices can only be issued for amounts up to £250 including VAT	
A customer cannot use a pro-forma invoice to reclaim input tax	

2.8 Charles runs a lighting shop. He buys 16 lamps from the wholesaler for £27.50 each including VAT at the standard rate. How much VAT will be included on the invoice from the wholesaler?

Select **one** option.

£88	
£73.33	
£5.50	
£4.58	

2.9 Marina is preparing an invoice for a customer for standard-rated goods (standard rate is 20%). The customer is entitled to a 10% trade discount. The list price of the goods is £220. What is the total VAT to be shown on the invoice?

Select **one** option.

£44	
£39.60	
£36.66	
£33	

2.10 Dolby Ltd supplies standard-rated goods to a customer at a price of £1,500 excluding VAT. The terms of the sale are that the customer will receive a prompt payment discount of 8% if they pay within 10 days. The customer pays the invoice within seven days.

How much output tax should Dolby Ltd include in its VAT account for this supply?

£ [ ]

2.11 The business that you work for receives an invoice for £271.68, which includes VAT at 20%. What is the net amount of the invoice, and the VAT included?

Select **one** option.

Net invoice amount is £226.40, and the VAT included is £45.28	
Net invoice amount is £217.35, and the VAT included is £54.33	
Net invoice amount is £271.68, and the VAT included is £54.33	
Net invoice amount is £271.68, and the VAT included is £45.28	

2.12 Malcolm is registered for VAT and issues an invoice for plumbing services with a standard price of £440. He offers a trade discount to regular customers. The total amount including standard-rated VAT shown on the invoice to a regular customer is £475.20. What is the rate of discount that has been given?

Select **one** option.

7.4%	
8%	
10%	
12%	

2.13 Ezra is the proprietor of a VAT-registered business. On 10 July he receives an order from a customer for standard VAT-rated goods. He delivers the goods to the customer on 12 July and issues an invoice on 16 July. The customer pays the invoice on 24 July. What is the tax point for this invoice?

Select **one** option.

10 July	
12 July	
16 July	
24 July	

2.14   On 25 June, Jamie placed an order for goods costing £1,200 including standard-rated VAT and paid a deposit of £300 on 1 July. The goods were delivered to Jamie on 7 July, and the supplier issued an invoice for the goods on 14 July. Jamie paid the balance of £900 on 25 July. What are the tax points for the deposit and the balance?

Select **one** date for each.

	Deposit	Balance
25 June		
1 July		
7 July		
14 July		
25 July		

2.15   Enrique runs a VAT-registered business. A new customer orders standard-rated goods with a list price of £5,000. Enrique issues a pro-forma invoice dated 29 September. Payment for the goods is received on 3 October and the goods are delivered to the customer on 5 October. Enrique issues a VAT invoice to the customer on 6 October. What is the tax point for this invoice?

Select **one** option.

29 September	
3 October	
5 October	
6 October	

2.16   HMRC publishes a VAT fraction to calculate the VAT included in a total amount. When the VAT rate is 20%, what is the VAT fraction?

4/5	
2/3	
1/5	
1/6	

3 Inputs and outputs and special schemes

3.1 Arnold runs a VAT-registered business that sells a mix of zero-rated and standard-rated goods. Which of the following statements is true of Arnold's business?

Select **one** option.

Arnold can reclaim all the input VAT charged to his business	
The amount of input VAT that Arnold can reclaim will be subject to 'de minimis' rules	
Arnold can only claim back the input VAT that relates to the standard-rated goods that he sells	
None of the input VAT can be reclaimed by Arnold's business	

3.2 A VAT-registered business supplies only zero-rated goods. The majority of the business's inputs are standard-rated for VAT. Which of the following will be true of the VAT Returns made by this business?

Select **one** option.

Most of the business's VAT Returns will result in an amount payable to HMRC	
The business will rarely have to complete a VAT Return as it supplies only zero-rated goods and so never has to pay money to HMRC	
The business will only have to complete a VAT Return if it starts to supply standard-rated goods	
Most of the business's VAT Returns will result in a repayment from HMRC	

3.3   A business has made £160,000 of supplies in a VAT quarter. Out of this, £40,000 were VATable supplies and the remainder were VAT-exempt. What proportion of the residual input VAT can be claimed back on the business's VAT Return?

Select **one** option.

100%	
75%	
25%	
0%	

3.4   JRB & Co is a VAT-registered business which only supplies standard-rated services. The finance assistant is preparing the VAT Return. He has a query over three invoices which all include VAT at 20%:

- £230 for staff entertaining
- £450 for a laptop computer
- £329 for entertaining a client based in the UK.

What is the total input VAT that JRB & Co can claim for these invoices on its VAT Return?

Select **one** option.

£93.16	
£113.33	
£129.83	
£168.16	

3.5   Juno is a plumber who is registered for VAT. He has recently refitted the bathroom at his home and has taken goods out of the business with a list price of £300 that actually cost him £270. Had he used them in his business, he would have charged the customer £390 (all figures exclude VAT).

What is the total amount including VAT that Juno should treat as drawings?

Select **one** option.

£468	
£360	
£324	
None	

3.6   Decide whether the following statement is true or false.

'The VAT on the cost of entertaining UK clients can be treated as an allowable input tax, whereas the VAT on staff entertainment cannot.'

TRUE / FALSE

3.7   Albatross Ltd, a VAT-registered business, bought a brand new company car four years ago for £20,000 plus VAT. The company correctly reclaimed the input VAT at the time the car was purchased. Albatross Ltd has agreed to sell the car to a private individual. Decide which of the following statements is true.

Select **one** option.

Output VAT should be charged on the sale of the car as the input VAT on its purchase was reclaimed by Albatross Ltd	
Output VAT should not be charged on the sale of the car as the individual is not VAT-registered	
Output VAT should not be charged on the sale of the car because it is more than three years old	
Output VAT should not be charged on the sale of the car because the standard rate of VAT has changed in the last four years	

3.8 A business purchases fuel that will be used for both business and private motoring. The business does not wish to keep detailed records of business and private mileage. Complete the following statement.

'The business can reclaim all the VAT charged and then pay [ ] to HMRC which is based on the CO_2 emissions of the vehicle.'

3.9 For each of the VAT-registered businesses in the table below, decide whether input tax can be recovered, is blocked, or is partially blocked.

Where appropriate, calculate the amount of input tax that can be recovered.

	Input tax can be recovered	Input tax blocked	Input tax partially blocked	Input tax that can be recovered
	✔	✔	✔	£
Jojo is a driving instructor who leases a car for her business. The monthly lease cost is £329.70, including VAT at 20%				
Sami is a farmer who has purchased a second-hand tractor for £37,230, plus VAT at the standard rate				
Jenensi Ltd leases a car for its training manager. The monthly lease cost is £612.60, including VAT at 20%				
Honor is a self-employed florist. She uses a van solely to deliver flowers to customers. She has recently had the van serviced which cost £420 including VAT				

3.10 Mearse Ltd provides a company car to its finance director. The business has paid for all the car's fuel since it was purchased, including VAT at standard rate. The car has CO_2 emissions of 187 g/km.

Mearse Ltd reclaims all the VAT on the fuel, and accounts for private fuel used by the sales manager using the appropriate fuel scale charge. Which of these is the correct fuel scale charge for the VAT quarter ending 31 January 2024?

Select **one** option.

£164	
£497	
£515	
£1,988	

3.11 The following conditions apply to a business operating one of the special accounting schemes available in the UK:

- Annual taxable turnover is £800,000

- Payments are made to HMRC four times a year

- VAT Returns are submitted once a year

Which of the following schemes is being used?

Flat rate scheme	
Cash accounting scheme	
Annual accounting scheme	

3.12 Andrew is registered for the flat rate VAT scheme, and the flat rate for his business is 7.5%. In the last quarter the following sales and purchases were made:

Standard-rated sales (including VAT at 20%)	£26,088
Zero-rated sales	£4,944
Purchases (including VAT at 20%)	£11,240

What is the VAT payable by Andrew's business for the quarter?

Select **one** option.

£2,327.40	
£1,956.60	
£1,484.40	
£1,113.60	

3.13 Complete the following statement.

'A business can operate the cash accounting scheme for VAT in conjunction with the

[ ] accounting scheme for VAT, but not with the [ ] accounting

scheme for VAT.'

3.14   Which of the following businesses would most benefit from registering for the cash accounting scheme?

Select **one** option.

A business that is given 45 days credit by its suppliers, but which receives payment from its customers in cash	
A business that pays its suppliers in cash but allows its customers 60 days credit	
A business that makes all its sales and purchases in cash	
A business that makes all its sales and purchases on 30 days credit	

3.15   Comsten Ltd operates the annual accounting scheme. The best estimate of its VAT liability for the next year is £89,100. What is the business's payment on account schedule for this tax year?

Select **one** option.

Three payments of £29,700 paid in months 4, 7 and 10	
Four payments of £22,275 paid in months 3, 6, 9 and 12	
Nine payments of £8,910 paid in months 4 to 12 with a balancing payment in month 14	
Nine payments of £990 paid in months 4 to 12 with a balancing payment in month 13	

3.16   James is a self-employed writer who produces articles for educational websites and online publications. He does not have an office and works from home. His turnover is £91,100 excluding VAT, and his costs of goods are £2,050 including VAT.

If James has registered for the flat rate scheme, what rate of VAT must he use?

Select **one** option.

20%	
16.5%	
5%	
0%	

3.17 Ramona runs a carpentry business and operates the flat rate for VAT. She has just sold an electric plane that she no longer has use for in the business, for £1,200. Ramona originally bought the plane two years ago for £4,200, including VAT, and claimed the input VAT paid on it at the time of purchase.

How much VAT must Ramona pay to HMRC on the sale of the electric plane?

Select **one** option.

£700	
£500	
£200	
£0	

3.18 Decide whether the following statement is true or false.

'If an overseas customer asks for goods to be delivered to a UK address, the goods cannot be zero-rated for VAT.'

TRUE / FALSE

3.19 Mylo has bought a laptop for £1,332, including standard rate VAT. He will use it 70% of the time for his business, and the remainder for personal use. How much input VAT can Mylo reclaim on the asset?

Select **one** option.

£222.00	
£155.40	
£66.60	
£0	

4 The VAT Return, errors, and penalties

4.1 Vernon has completed his VAT Return for the quarter ended 30 September. The figure in Box 3 is £45,324 and the figure in Box 4 is £52,796. This will result in which of the following?

Select **one** option.

Vernon will have to pay HMRC £7,472	
Vernon will reclaim £7,472 from HMRC	
Vernon will have to pay HMRC £45,324	
Vernon will reclaim £52,796 from HMRC	

4.2 All supplies made by a business are taxable at the reduced rate of VAT. The business offers a 5% trade discount, and this quarter all the sales recorded in the sales daybook have been made to trade customers. If the list price of sales for the quarter is £65,342.88, excluding VAT, how much output tax will be posted from the sales daybook to the VAT control account?

Select **one** option.

£13,068.57	
£12,415.14	
£3,267.14	
£3,103.78	

4.3 Lanuka Ltd discovers a genuine error in its VAT records. An invoice dated 17 August 2023 was issued to a customer showing output tax of £76.94. However, the figure should have been £769.40. The VAT Return for the quarter ended 31 December 2023 shows output tax of £35,345.

What will be the final figure for output tax on Lanuka Ltd's VAT Return for the quarter ended 31 December 2023?

£ _____

4.4   Ravi has entered the details of a sale made to a new customer into the accounting software. The total amount owed by the customer, including standard rate VAT at 20%, is £407.40. However, the accounting software has calculated the VAT included in the invoice as £19.40. Which two of the following statements are correct?

Select **two** options.

The accounting software has correctly calculated the VAT on the invoice at reduced rate	
The accounting software has correctly calculated the VAT on the invoice at the standard rate	
The accounting software has incorrectly calculated the VAT on the invoice at reduced rate	
Ravi needs to adjust the VAT rate for the customer in the accounting software	

4.5   A business discovers that a net error has been made on its VAT Return.

In which of the following circumstances will the business **not** be required to make a voluntary disclosure?

Select **one** option.

The net error is £10,294, and the quarterly turnover is £485,450	
The net error is £14,234, and the quarterly turnover is £300,000	
The net error is £8,435, and the quarterly turnover is £83,200	
The net error is £13,222, and the quarterly turnover is £1,200,000	

4.6   Rogers Ltd has completed its VAT Return for the current quarter, which correctly shows an amount of £27,451 payable to HMRC. Rogers Ltd made a payment of £22,948 to HMRC for the previous quarter. Unfortunately, this amount has been entered into the VAT account on the wrong side.

What is the uncorrected balance currently shown on the VAT control account?

Select **one** option.

An amount payable to HMRC of £50,399	
An amount payable to HMRC of £73,347	
An amount receivable from HMRC of £4,503	
An amount receivable from HMRC of £50,399	

4.7   Milly has identified an error that she made in the previous quarter's VAT Return. She has omitted a sales invoice to a customer for £2,740, plus VAT at standard rate.

(a)   How much will the adjustment need to be for this error in the current quarter's VAT Return?

£ [   ]

(b)   This adjustment will [   ] on the VAT Return.

Select **one** of the following options to complete the sentence:

increase input tax; increase output tax; decrease input tax; decrease output tax

4.8   Hapeful Ltd has discovered that one of its customers has gone into liquidation owing the business £4,238.40, including standard rate VAT, and it will not receive any of the money owed. The debt is over six months old, and Hapeful Ltd has written it off in its accounts. How much bad debt relief can the business claim for this on its next VAT Return?

£ [   ]

4.9 For each of the following items decide whether it will be a debit or a credit in a business's VAT control account.

Select Debit VAT account, or Credit VAT account, for each item.

	Debit VAT Control account	Credit VAT Control account
VAT figure from the purchases daybook		
Bad debt relief		
VAT on cash sales		
VAT figure from the sales daybook		
VAT on items in the petty cash book		

4.10 Desmond has been chasing payment from one of his customers and is now convinced that the customer will never pay. He wishes to claim bad debt relief on the invoice. Decide which of the following is **not** an HMRC requirement for a valid claim for bad debt relief.

Select **one** option.

The invoice must be more than six months overdue	
The debt must have been written off in Desmond's accounts	
The customer must have gone into liquidation	
Desmond must have paid the VAT on the invoice to HMRC	

4.11 The introduction of Making Tax Digital has replaced the VAT threshold so that all businesses that make VATable supplies must now submit a VAT Return regardless of their annual turnover.

TRUE / FALSE

4.12   Meera owns and runs a cleaning business. Every month she takes household products for use in her own home, costing £65, plus VAT at standard rate. How should Meera treat this in her next quarterly VAT Return?

Select **one** option.

Include £78 in Box 1 of her VAT Return	
Include £234 in Box 1 of her VAT Return	
Include £39 in Box 1 of her VAT Return	
She does not need to do anything as it is her business	

4.13   Decide whether the following sentence is true or false.

'A business that has been registered for VAT for several years, with annual turnover of £115,000, has submitted its latest quarterly VAT Return late for the first time. In this situation the business will receive a late submission penalty point.'

TRUE / FALSE

4.14   Linkaway Ltd started trading on 1 June 2023. It registered for VAT on 1 July as it predicted its turnover in the next 12 months would exceed the registration threshold in the next 12 months.

The owners of the business did not know when its first VAT Return for the quarter ended 30 September was due, and only submitted it on 1 January 2024.

(a)   What was the due date for the VAT Return for the quarter ended 30 September 2023?

30 September 2023	
7 October 2023	
10 October 2023	
31 October 2023	
7 November 2023	

(b)   How many late submission penalty points will Linkaway Ltd receive for submitting this VAT Return late?

Four points	
Three points	
One point	
Zero points	

(c)   If Linkaway Ltd submits its next quarterly VAT Return late, how much will the penalty payment be?

£0	
£100	
£200	
£400	

4.15   Rebemma Ltd submits its VAT Returns quarterly, and always submits them on time. However, it has not made its last two payments of VAT due to HMRC for the VAT quarter ending 31 July 2023, and 31 October 2023.

Today's date is 5 January 2024.

Complete the table below to show the date the second VAT payment was due (the first has been given), the number of days each VAT payment is overdue, and the first and second late payments penalties due to HMRC for each late payment, to the nearest whole £.

VAT Quarter ended:	VAT amount due	Date VAT due to HMRC	Number of days payment overdue	First late payment penalty	Second late payment penalty
				£	£
31 July 2023	£9,700	7 September 2023			
31 October 2023	£8,500				

4.16   Jilly Greentrees runs her own VAT-registered personal training business, Jump with Jilly Ltd. The business is a limited cost business on the flat rate scheme for VAT, and therefore uses a flat rate percentage of 16.5%.

In the last quarter Jilly paid HMRC £3,772.25.

Jilly has recently moved to a new accounting software package.

Total sales for the current quarter, including standard rate VAT, are £33,250, so Jilly expects to pay HMRC £5,486.25.

The draft VAT Return produced by new accounting software, shows that she needs to pay £6,528.40.

Jilly's purchases for the quarter were £608 including standard rate VAT.

Which of the following has caused the difference between what Jilly expected to pay, and what the accounting software says is due to HMRC?

Select **one** option.

The accounting software has been correctly set up for the normal VAT scheme	
The accounting software has been set up with a flat rate of 12%	
The accounting software has been incorrectly set up for the cash accounting scheme for VAT	
The accounting software has been incorrectly set up for the normal VAT scheme	

4.17   Identify whether each of the following transactions should be included in Box 1 or Box 4 of a quarterly VAT Return, or both.

	Box 1	Box 4	Boxes 1 & 4
VAT on bad debt relief			
VAT on a credit note received from a supplier			
VAT on goods taken by a business owner for personal use			
Fuel scale charges			
VAT on a purchase invoice omitted in error from the previous quarter's VAT Return			
VAT due on imports accounted for through postponed VAT accounting			

4.18   This question is about preparing figures for a business's VAT Return for the quarter ended 30 September 2023.

The standard rate of VAT is 20%.

The following accounts have been extracted from the ledgers:

Sales account

Date 2023	Reference	Debit £	Date 2023	Reference	Credit £
30/09	Balance c/d	401,370.00	01/07 – 30/09	Sales daybook – UK sales	248,950.00
			01/07 – 30/09	Sales daybook – exports	56,000.00
			01/07 – 30/09	Cash book – UK sales	96,420.00
	Total	401,370.00		Total	401,370.00

Purchases account

Date 2023	Reference	Debit £	Date 2023	Reference	Credit £
01/07 -30/09	Purchases daybook – UK purchases	145,654.00	30/09	Balance c/d	167,854.00
01/07 -30/09	Purchases daybook – zero-rated imports	22,200.00			
	Total	167,854.00		Total	167,854.00

VAT account

Date 2023	Reference	Debit £	Date 2023	Reference	Credit £
01/07 -30/09	Purchases daybook – UK purchases	29,130.80	01/07 -30/09	Sales daybook – UK sales	49,790.00
			01/07 -30/09	Cash book – UK sales	19,284.00

You are told that bad debt relief on a sales invoice for £948.75 excluding VAT is to be claimed in this quarter.

(a) Calculate the figure to be claimed as bad debt relief on the VAT Return.

£ [   ]

(b) Calculate the figure for Box 1 of the VAT Return – VAT due on sales and other outputs.

£ [   ]

(c) Calculate the figure for Box 4 of the VAT Return.

£ [   ]

5 Principles of payroll

5.1 Identify whether each of the following statements is true or false.

	True	False
Registration as an employer must be at least two months before employees are first paid		
The online process for transmitting payroll information to HMRC is called Real Time Information		
Payroll information must be kept for six years after the end of the tax year to which they relate		
Payroll information can be held electronically		

5.2 Niles left his employment at Rollo Ltd on 31 March. It is now 18 December, and the Human Resources Manager has discovered that the business is still holding personal data about Miles including his bank account details.

State which of the data protection principles Rollo Ltd is breaching by continuing to hold this information.

5.3 The number element of an employee's tax code is multiplied by what number to give the employee's personal allowance?

5.4 Identify whether each of the following statements is true or false.

	True	False
Student loans are not a statutory deduction from gross pay		
Contribution to a company pension scheme does not reduce an employee's taxable pay		
Payroll giving to charity reduces an employee's taxable pay		
Class 1 National Insurance Contributions are normally paid by an employee once their earnings exceed £184 per week		
Class 1A and Class 1B National Insurance Contributions are paid by the employer		

5.5 Complete the following sentence about workplace pensions:

To enrol in a workplace pension scheme, an employee must be classified as a worker, and be aged between ⬚ years old and state pension age. They must earn at least £ ⬚ .

The employer must pay a minimum of ⬚ % of the employee's total earnings into the pension scheme, and the employee must pay a minimum of ⬚ %.

5.6 Which of these forms is provided to an employee when they leave an employment?

Select **one** option.

P11D	
Payslip	
P60	
P45	

5.7   What is the maximum reduction in its annual Class 1 NIC an employer can get if it is eligible for Employment Allowance?

Select **one** option.

£5,000	
£48,000	
£120,000	

5.8   Details of new employees, or employees who leave, will be included on which of these forms and submitted to HMRC?

Select **one** option.

Full Payment Submission	
Employer Payment Summary	

5.9   Complete the following sentence about P11D forms.

An employer submits P11D forms online to HMRC by ⬚ after the end of the tax year to which they relate. It must then pay any Class 1A National Insurance Contributions by ⬚.

5.10   Complete the following sentence about P60 forms.

If an employee is working for an employer on 5 April, the employer must provide P60 forms to employees by ⬚.

5.11 Which of the following are non-statutory deductions from an employee's gross pay?

Select **all** options that apply.

Pension contributions	
Student loans	
Union membership fees	
Charitable giving	
National Insurance Contributions	
Private medical insurance	
Savings schemes	
Income Tax	

5.12 Frederick runs a business with 37 employees. He has deliberately paid some of his employees in cash for overtime hours, and only declared their basic working hours in his payroll submission. Frederick has now informed HMRC of this situation.

What is the maximum percentage of lost revenue (PLR) that HMRC can charge Frederick in this situation?

Select **one** option.

20%	
30%	
70%	
100%	

5.13   Fixxo Ltd, a manufacturing business in the UK with 187 employees, has failed to file its Employer Payment Summary (EPS) on time for the third time this tax year. What will be the total penalty for this?

Select **one** option.

£200	
£300	
£600	
£900	

5.14   Wassim works as an accountant at Crofter Ltd. He has prepared the wages report for the October payroll, which is paid to employees on 27 October, an extract from which is shown below:

	£
Gross wages	91,742.10
Income Tax	6,471.50
Employers' NIC	9,721.25
Employees' NIC	10,113.01

Complete the following information about the payroll information

The amount due to HMRC is ……	
The date the amount must be paid by is ….	
The form that the calculations of the employers' National Insurance Contributions will be shown on is the …….	

5.15 Sammi joined Fethers Ltd on 12 August 2023. He has been given his P60 by his employer, and is confused, as the amount shown does not agree with what he actually received in the tax year 2023/24 from Fethers Ltd, which was £20,220.71.

His P60 shows the following information:

Pay and Income Tax details		£
	Pay £	Tax deducted £
In previous employment(s)	13,210.01	1,759.62
In this employment	26,214.20	3,611.22
Total for the year	39,424.21	5,370.84

Employee's National Insurance in this employment	2,382.27

Complete the reconciliation below to explain to Sammi why the amount he has received differs from the amount on his P60.

	£
Amounts received	20,220.71
Amount per P60 in 2023/24	

6 Communicating VAT and payroll information

6.1 A colleague who you work with in a VAT-registered business tells you that she needs to contact HMRC about a VAT matter. She asks you what she should do in this situation. Decide in which order she should take each of the following actions by ranking them 1st, 2nd, or 3rd.

	Ranking
Write to HMRC	
Telephone the HMRC helpline	
Visit the HMRC website	

6.2 Decide whether the following statement is true or false.

'Because you submit your VAT Return online then you are only permitted to communicate with HMRC via email.'

TRUE / FALSE

6.3 A professional accountant who is responsible for completing the business's VAT Return should ensure that he keeps himself fully up-to-date with current VAT regulations in order to comply with which of the following fundamental ethical principles?

Select **one** option.

Confidentiality	
Professional competence and due care	
Objectivity	
Professional behaviour	

6.4   The owner of the business that you work for has given you a receipt for £1,800 for carpet and fitting. He has asked you to process it through the business's accounts and reclaim the VAT in the usual way. When you look at the invoice closely you notice that the carpet has been fitted at the owner's home.

Which of the following is the ethical approach to take in this situation?

Explain to the owner that as this is personal expenditure it is disallowed for VAT so the VAT cannot be reclaimed	
Immediately report the owner of the business to HMRC	

6.5   Kirsten works as an assistant accountant at Edwards and Sons Ltd. She has prepared the draft VAT Return for the business for the quarter ended 31 January 2024. She needs to inform the finance manager before submitting the VAT Return.

A summary of the figures extracted from the accounting software is shown here:

	£
Output VAT	11,022.20
Input VAT	7,741.89
Outputs	85,047
Inputs	55,111

(a)   Complete the following information that Kirsten should include in an email to the finance manager before the VAT Return is submitted.

The VAT Return must be submitted to HMRC by ….	
The amount due to HMRC is ….	
HMRC will collect this amount by direct debit on ….	

(b)   Kirsten has been talking to some of her fellow students at college and thinks that there are lots of advantages to Edwards & Sons Ltd moving to cash accounting for VAT. What should she do with this information?

Select **one** option.

Ask HMRC to move the business to cash accounting for VAT	
Ask one of her fellow students to help her move the business to cash accounting for VAT	
Prepare a brief report for the finance manager summarising the benefits to the business of moving to cash accounting for VAT	
Do nothing, this is not part of her job role	

6.6 You are an Accounting Technician who works for a chain of clothing shops, and you report to the Chief Finance Officer. You have been asked to advise him on how an increase in the rate of VAT would affect the business and what action would have to be taken as a consequence.

Today's date is 15 October.

Prepare a draft email to the Chief Finance Officer providing information about some of the potential effects and consequences of a change. Choose **ONE** option to complete each sentence.

To:	**(Accounting technician/Chief finance officer)**
From:	**(Accounting technician/Chief finance officer)**
Date:	15 October

When the rate of VAT changes, the business must consider whether the prices it charges to customers will change. These prices **cannot change until the date of the next VAT Return / must change on the date of the VAT change / can remain unchanged if the business chooses**.

The new rate of VAT must be reflected in the amount of VAT paid to HMRC **only if we change the prices to customers / whether we change the prices to customers or not / only if customers choose to pay the new prices**.

If the date of the VAT change falls during one of our VAT periods, our system must **apply a single rate of VAT during that VAT period / apply dual rates of VAT during that VAT period depending on the customer / apply dual rates of VAT during that VAT period depending on each sale transaction's tax point**.

Kind regards

A Technician

6.7 You have just produced the quarterly VAT Return for the quarter ended 31 May using the business's accounting software. The owner of the business is responsible for the day-to-day running of the business, but uses an external firm of accountants to prepare the financial statements at the year-end. Who should you send the VAT Return to prior to submitting it electronically on the gov.uk website?

HMRC	
The owner of the business	
The external accountants	
No one as you are submitting the return using a digital link	

6.8   The business that you work for operates the flat rate scheme for VAT and is not a limited cost business. One of your fellow students who works in a similar business has told you that the flat rate percentage has increased by 1%. She says any business may be liable to a penalty if it uses the wrong flat rate percentage. Which of the following sources would you use to find out the correct information about whether the flat rate has changed?

Select **all** options that apply.

Discussion with the human resources manager	
Update on the gov.uk website	
Further discussions with the other trainee accountant	
Information from the external accountants	

Answers to chapter activities

1 Introduction to Value Added Tax

1.1

Income Tax	
Input tax	
Output tax	✔
Sales tax	

1.2   FALSE

1.3

It will have no effect on the VAT payable by the business	
It will increase the amount of VAT due to be paid	✔
It will decrease the amount of VAT due to be paid	

1.4

It will increase the VAT payable by £20	
It will decrease the VAT payable by £20	✔
It will increase the VAT payable by £112	
It will decrease the VAT payable by £112	

1.5

All £160 is paid over to HMRC by the customer	
All £160 is paid over to HMRC by the retailer	
The retailer pays £60, and the manufacturer pays £100 to HMRC	✔
The manufacturer pays the whole £160 to HMRC	

1.6

0%	
5%	✔
17.5%	
20%	

1.7

It only supplies standard-rated products	
Whilst it previously supplied standard-rated products it now only supplies products that attract reduced rate VAT	
The owner of the business is winding the business down prior to retiring	✔
The business only supplies zero-rated products	

1.8

A business that only supplies products which are exempt from VAT	
An individual who sells his/her own second-hand clothing on eBay	
A business that annually supplies standard-rated goods with a list price of £47,000 p.a.	✔
A business that supplies exempt goods with a list price of £98,000	

1.9

A VAT Return	
Certificate of registration	✔
Trading certificate	
VAT control account	

1.10

2025	
2027	
2029	✔
2030	

1.11

20% of potential lost revenue	
50% of potential lost revenue	
70% of potential lost revenue	✔
100% of potential lost revenue	

1.12 TRUE

1.13 FALSE

1.14

30 April 2024	
31 October 2024	
30 November 2024	✔
1 April 2025	

1.15 January 2024

2   VAT and business documents

2.1

	Must be included on a full VAT invoice
Customer order number	
Invoice date	✔
Description of the goods or services supplied	✔
Customer's VAT number	
Seller's VAT number	✔
Customer name and address	✔
Seller's name and address	✔
Seller's required payment method	
Rate of prompt payment discount (if offered)	✔
VAT rates applied	✔
Amount excluding VAT	✔
Amount of VAT charged	✔

2.2

The invoice should only show the total VAT charges	
The invoice should show the standard rate VAT and the reduced rate VAT as separate amounts on the invoice	✔
The invoice should show the standard rate VAT separately and include the reduced rate VAT in the Gross amount due	
The invoice should show the reduced rate VAT separately and include the standard rate VAT in the Gross amount due	

2.3   'A business can issue a simplified invoice if the amount charged for the supply, including VAT, is **£250,** or less.'

2.4

The business can issue a simplified invoice as the total supplies including VAT are less than £250	
The business can issue a simplified invoice as the total supplies excluding VAT are less than £250	
The business cannot issue a simplified invoice as the invoice includes exempt supplies	✔
Simplified invoices cannot be issued if there are mixed supplies	

2.5

£20	
£97	
£100	
£120	
£217	✔

2.6 **(a)**

15 November	✔
22 November	
30 November	
20 December	

(b) £540

2.7

	True about a pro-forma invoice
Pro-forma invoices must show the supplier's VAT registration number	✔
Pro-forma invoices are normally used to collect payment from a customer prior to supplying the goods	✔
Pro-forma invoices can only be issued for amounts up to £250 including VAT	
A customer cannot use a pro-forma invoice to reclaim input tax	✔

2.8

£88	
£73.33	✔
£5.50	
£4.58	

2.9

£44	
£39.60	✔
£36.66	
£33	

2.10   £276

Workings: £1,500 x 92% x 20%

2.11

Net invoice amount is £226.40, and the VAT included is £45.28	✔
Net invoice amount is £217.35, and the VAT included is £54.33	
Net invoice amount is £271.68, and the VAT included is £54.33	
Net invoice amount is £271.68, and the VAT included is £45.28	

2.12

7.4%	
8%	
10%	✔
12%	

Workings: £475.20 ÷ 120% = £396

£440 – £396 = £44 discount

(£44 ÷ £440) x 100% = 10%

2.13

10 July	
12 July	
16 July	✔
24 July	

2.14

	Deposit	Balance
25 June		
1 July	✔	
7 July		
14 July		✔
25 July		

2.15

29 September	
3 October	✔
5 October	
6 October	

2.16

4/5	
2/3	
1/5	
1/6	✔

3 Inputs and outputs and special schemes

3.1

Arnold can reclaim all the input VAT charged to his business	✔
The amount of input VAT that Arnold can reclaim will be subject to 'de minimis' rules	
Arnold can only claim back the input VAT that relates to the standard-rated goods that he sells	
None of the input VAT can be reclaimed by Arnold's business	

3.2

Most of the business's VAT Returns will result in an amount payable to HMRC	
The business will rarely have to complete a VAT Return as it supplies only zero-rated goods and so never has to pay money to HMRC	
The business will only have to complete a VAT Return if it starts to supply standard-rated goods	
Most of the business's VAT Returns will result in a repayment from HMRC	✔

3.3

100%	
75%	
25%	✔
0%	

3.4

£93.16	
£113.33	✔
£129.83	
£168.16	

3.5

£468	
£360	
£324	✔
None	

3.6 FALSE. The VAT on the cost of staff entertainment can be treated as an allowable input tax, whereas the VAT on client entertainment cannot.

3.7

Output VAT should be charged on the sale of the car as the input VAT on its purchase was reclaimed by Albatross Ltd	✔
Output VAT should not be charged on the sale of the car as the individual is not VAT-registered	
Output VAT should not be charged on the sale of the car because it is more than three years old	
Output VAT should not be charged on the sale of the car because the standard rate of VAT has changed in the last four years	

3.8 'The business can reclaim all the VAT charged and then pay **fuel scale charge** to HMRC which is based on the CO_2 emissions of the vehicle.'

3.9

	Input tax can be recovered	Input tax blocked	Input tax partially blocked	Input tax that can be recovered £
Jojo is a driving instructor who leases a car for her business. The monthly lease cost is £329.70, including VAT at 20%	✔			54.95
Sami is a farmer who has purchased a second-hand tractor for £37,230, plus VAT at the standard rate	✔			7,446.00
Jenensi Ltd leases a car for its training manager. The monthly lease cost is £612.60, including VAT at 20%			✔	51.05
Honor is a self-employed florist. She uses a van solely to deliver flowers to customers. She has recently had the van serviced which cost £420 including VAT	✔			70.00

3.10

£164	
£497	✔
£515	
£1,988	

3.11

Flat rate scheme	
Cash accounting scheme	
Annual accounting scheme	✔

3.12

£2,327.40	✔
£1,956.60	
£1,484.40	
£1,113.60	

3.13 'A business can operate the cash accounting scheme in conjunction with the **annual** accounting scheme but not with the **flat rate** accounting scheme.'

3.14

A business that is given 45 days credit by its suppliers, but which receives payment from its customers in cash	
A business that pays its suppliers in cash but allows its customers 60 days credit	✔
A business that makes all its sales and purchases in cash	
A business that makes all its sales and purchases on 30 days credit	

3.15

Three payments of £29,700 paid in months 4, 7 and 10	
Four payments of £22,275 paid in months 3, 6, 9 and 12	
Nine payments of £8,910 paid in months 4 to 12 with a balancing payment in month 14	✔
Nine payments of £990 paid in months 4 to 12 with a balancing payment in month 13	

3.16

20%	
16.5%	✔
5%	
0%	

3.17

£700	
£500	
£200	✔
£0	

3.18 TRUE - If an overseas customer asks for goods to be delivered to a UK address the goods cannot be zero-rated for VAT.

3.19

£222.00	
£155.40	✔
£66.60	
£0	

4 The VAT Return

4.1

Vernon will have to pay HMRC £7,472	
Vernon will reclaim £7,472 from HMRC	✔
Vernon will have to pay HMRC £45,324	
Vernon will reclaim £52,796 from HMRC	

4.2

£13,068.57	
£12,415.14	
£3,267.14	
£3,103.78	✔

4.3   £36,037.46

4.4

The accounting software has correctly calculated the VAT on the invoice at reduced rate	
The accounting software has correctly calculated the VAT on the invoice at the standard rate	
The accounting software has incorrectly calculated the VAT on the invoice at reduced rate	✔
Ravi needs to adjust the VAT rate for the customer in the accounting software	✔

4.5

The net error is £10,294, and the quarterly turnover is £485,450	
The net error is £14,234, and the quarterly turnover is £300,000	
The net error is £8,435, and the quarterly turnover is £83,200	✔
The net error is £13,222, and the quarterly turnover is £1,200,000	

4.6

An amount payable to HMRC of £50,399	
An amount payable to HMRC of £73,347	✔
An amount receivable from HMRC of £4,503	
An amount receivable from HMRC of £50,399	

4.7 **(a)** £548

(b) This adjustment will **increase output tax** on the VAT Return.

4.8 £706.40

4.9

	Debit VAT account	Credit VAT account
VAT figure from the purchases daybook	✔	
Bad debt relief	✔	
VAT on cash sales		✔
VAT figure from the sales daybook		✔
VAT on items in the petty cash book	✔	

4.10

The invoice must be more than six months overdue	
The debt must have been written off in Desmond's accounts	
The customer must have gone into liquidation	✔
Desmond must have paid the VAT on the invoice to HMRC	

4.11 FALSE. Making Tax Digital governs the way in which VAT Returns are submitted to HMRC. The VAT threshold still determines whether a business must register for VAT or not.

4.12

Include £78 in Box 1 of her VAT Return	
Include £234 in Box 1 of her VAT Return	
Include £39 in Box 1 of her VAT Return	✔
She does not need to do anything as it is her business	

4.13 TRUE. The business with receive a late penalty point in this situation.

4.14 (a)

30 September 2023	
7 October 2023	
10 October 2023	
31 October 2023	
7 November 2023	✔

(b)

Four points	
Three points	
One point	
Zero points	✔

(c)

£0	✔
£100	
£200	
£400	

4.15

VAT Quarter ended:	VAT amount due	Date VAT due to HMRC	Number of days payment overdue	First late payment penalty £	Second late payment penalty £
31 July 2023	£9,700	7 September 2023	120 days	£9,700 x 4% = £388	£9,700 x 4% x (120 – 31)/365 = £94.61 ie £95
31 October 2023	£8,500	7 December 2023	29 days	£8,500 x 2% = £170	None

4.16

The accounting software has been correctly set up for the normal VAT scheme	
The accounting software has been set up with a flat rate of 12%	
The accounting software has been incorrectly set up for the cash accounting scheme for VAT	
The accounting software has been incorrectly set up for the normal VAT scheme	✔

4.17

	Box 1	Box 4	Boxes 1 & 4
VAT on bad debt relief		✔	
VAT on a credit note received from a supplier		✔	
VAT on goods taken by a business owner for personal use	✔		
Fuel scale charges	✔		
VAT on a purchase invoice omitted in error from the previous quarter's VAT return		✔	
VAT due on imports accounted for through postponed VAT accounting			✔

4.18 **(a)** £189.75

(b) £69,074

(c) £29,320.55

5   Principles of payroll

5.1

	True	False
Registration as an employer must be at least two months before employees are first paid		✔
The online process for transmitting payroll information to HMRC is called Real Time Information	✔	
Payroll information must be kept for six years after the end of the tax year to which they relate		✔
Payroll information can be held electronically	✔	

5.2   Organisations must ensure that information is kept for no longer than is necessary.

5.3   Multiplying the number element of an employee's tax code by **10** will give their personal allowance.

5.4

	True	False
Student loans are not a statutory deduction from gross pay		✔
Contribution to a company pension scheme does not reduce an employee's taxable pay		✔
Payroll giving to charity reduces an employee's taxable pay	✔	
Class 1 National Insurance Contributions are normally paid by an employee once their earnings exceed £184 per week	✔	
Class 1A and Class 1B National Insurance Contributions are paid by the employer	✔	

5.5   To enrol in a workplace pension scheme, an employee must be classified as a worker, and be aged between **22** years old and state pension age. They must earn at least **£10,000**.

The employer must pay a minimum of **3%** of the employee's total earnings into the pension scheme, and the employee must pay a minimum of **5%**.

5.6

P11D	
Payslip	
P60	
P45	✔

5.7

£5,000	✔
£48,000	
£120,000	

5.8

Full Payment Submission	✔
Employer Payment Summary	

5.9   An employer submits P11D forms online to HMRC by **6 July** after the end of the tax year to which they relate. It must then pay any Class 1A National Insurance Contributions by **22 July**.

5.10   If an employee is working for an employer on 5 April, the employer must provide P60 forms to employees by **31 May**.

5.11

Pension contributions	
Student loans	
Union membership fees	✔
Charitable giving	✔
National Insurance Contributions	
Private medical insurance	✔
Savings schemes	✔
Income Tax	

5.12

20%	
30%	
70%	
100%	✔

5.13

£200	
£300	
£600	✔
£900	

5.14

The amount due to HMRC is ……	£26,305.76
The date the amount must be paid by is ….	22 November
The form that the calculations of the employers' National Insurance Contributions will be shown on is the …….	FPS

5.15

	£
Amounts received	20,220.71
PAYE	3,611.22
Employee's National Insurance Contributions	2,382.27
Amount per P60 in 2023/24	26,214.20

6   Communicating VAT and payroll information

6.1

	Ranking
Write to HMRC	3
Telephone the HMRC helpline	2
Visit the HMRC website	1

6.2   FALSE. The method used to submit a VAT Return does not affect the way you can communicate with HMRC.

6.3

Confidentiality	
Professional competence and due care	✔
Objectivity	
Professional behaviour	

6.4

Explain to the owner that as this is personal expenditure it is disallowed for VAT so the VAT cannot be reclaimed	✔
Immediately report the owner of the business to HMRC	

6.5   **(a)**

The VAT Return must be submitted to HMRC by ….	7 March 2024
The amount due to HMRC is ….	£3,280.31
HMRC will collect this amount by direct debit on ….	10 March 2024

(b)

Ask HMRC to move the business to cash accounting for VAT	
Ask one of her fellow students to help her move the business to cash accounting for VAT	
Prepare a brief report for the finance manager summarising the benefits to the business of moving to cash accounting for VAT	✔
Do nothing, this is not part of her job role	

6.6

To: **Chief finance officer**

From: **Accounting technician**

Date: 15 October

When the rate of VAT changes, the business must consider whether the prices it charges to customers will change. These prices **can remain unchanged if the business chooses**.

The new rate of VAT must be reflected in the amount of VAT paid to HMRC **whether we change the prices to customers or not**.

If the date of the VAT change falls during one of our VAT periods, our system must **apply dual rates of VAT during that VAT period depending on each sale transaction's tax point**.

Kind regards

A Technician

6.7

HMRC	
The owner of the business	✔
The external accountants	
No one as you are submitting the return using a digital link	

6.8

Discussion with the human resources manager	
Update on the gov.uk website	✔
Further discussions with the other trainee accountant	
Information from the external accountants	✔

Practice
assessment 1

Task 1

This task is about understanding and calculating UK tax law principles relating to VAT, registration and deregistration and special schemes.

(a) Identify which of the following statements are correct about HMRC.

Select all options that apply.

HMRC is the tax authority for all taxes in the UK	
Businesses that only import goods from abroad are not regulated by HMRC	
HMRC will normally give businesses seven days' notice before a VAT visit	
HMRC is independent of the UK Government	

(b) During the year a business supplies goods that are a mixture of exempt, zero-rated and standard-rated. Over the next 12 months the business expects the split to be £25,000 exempt supplies, £30,000 zero-rated supplies, and £38,000 standard-rated supplies.

Which of the following statements is TRUE? Choose **one** answer.

The business will not have to register for VAT in the next year but can do so voluntarily	
The business will not be eligible to register for VAT at any point in the next year	
The business will be required to register for VAT at some point in the next year	

(c) The following conditions apply to a business operating a single special accounting scheme for VAT.

- The business has an annual taxable turnover of £920,000

- The business makes three interim payments each of 25% of its estimated VAT liability for the year

- The business submits one VAT Return for the year

Which of the following schemes is being used by the business? Choose **one** answer.

Flat rate scheme	
Cash accounting scheme	
Annual accounting scheme	

(d)   Complete the following statement by selecting **one** option.

A business with a short period of trading that temporarily takes it above the VAT registration threshold is permitted to remain unregistered provided it can prove that its turnover will fall below the threshold...

... almost immediately	
... within the next six months	
... within the next 12 months	

(e)   Decide which rate of VAT has been charged on each of the supplies below, by selecting one of the options below.

Options: exempt, zero rate, reduced rate, standard rate (use each one only once).

A business makes supplies of £120 including VAT of £20	
A business makes supplies of £225 on which no VAT can be charged	
A business makes supplies of £145 plus VAT of £7.25	
A business sends an invoice to a customer for £324.50 which states that the VAT is £nil	

Task 2

This task is about calculating and accounting for VAT.

(a)   A business that is registered for VAT is supplying standard-rated goods to a customer. The amount charged excluding VAT is £224.

Is the following statement true or false?

'The business may issue a simplified invoice.'

TRUE/FALSE

(b)   Shady Ltd sells car accessories on which VAT is charged at standard rate, and children's car seats and travel systems on which reduced rate VAT is charged.

Complete the following table to show the net amount, VAT, and gross amount, for each of the following supplies. Round your answers down to the nearest penny.

	Net £	VAT £	Gross £
Four car seat covers (standard rate VAT)	197.20		
Children's travel system (reduced rate VAT)			451.50
DAB radio (standard rate)		46.80	

(c)   The following information is available about an invoice issued by a business registered for VAT in the UK.

- A customer places an order with the business on 25 January and includes a 25% deposit with the order

- The business issues a VAT invoice for the deposit on 26 January

- The goods are delivered to the customer on 28 January together with an invoice for the remaining 75%

- The customer pays the invoice for the remaining 75% on 1 February

For VAT purposes what is/are the tax point(s) for this transaction?

Choose **one** answer.

The tax point for the deposit is 25 January and for the balance is 28 January	
The tax point for the deposit is 26 January and for the balance is 1 February	
The tax point for the deposit and the balance is 26 January	
The tax point for the deposit and the balance is 28 January	

(d)   A business despatches goods to a customer on 19 August. What is the latest date that the business is permitted to issue a VAT invoice for these goods?

Task 3

This task is about the recovery of input tax.

(a)   A business makes standard-rated, zero-rated, and exempt supplies. Decide which of the following statements is true regarding the business's input tax for the period.

Choose **one** answer.

If the exempt supplies exceed the 'de minimis' limit, all of the input tax can be reclaimed	
If the zero-rated supplies exceed the 'de minimis' limit, all of the input tax can be reclaimed	
If the exempt supplies are below the 'de minimis' limit, all of the input tax can be reclaimed	
If the zero-rated supplies are below the 'de minimis' limit, all of the input tax can be reclaimed	

(b)   A business does not currently operate any of the special accounting schemes. It wrote off an invoice on 12 September that was originally issued on 3 January, on 30 day credit terms. The invoice amount was £2,340 including VAT at standard rate. All the necessary conditions for claiming bad debt relief have been met by the business.

(i)   How much bad debt relief can be claimed by the business?

£ [   ]

(ii)   What is the earliest opportunity for the business to claim bad debt relief on this invoice?

Choose **one** answer.

In its VAT period ending 28 February	
In its VAT period ending 31 May	
In its VAT period ending 31 August	
In its VAT period ending 30 November	

(c) **(i)** Artigo Ltd bought a new company van four years ago. At the time of purchase Artigo Ltd correctly claimed the input VAT on the van. The business is now going to sell the van to a self-employed plumber who is not registered for VAT.

Which of the following statements is true? Choose **one** answer.

Artigo Ltd should charge output tax on the sale of the van because the plumber is going to use it solely for business purposes	
Artigo Ltd should charge output tax on the sale of the van because input VAT was claimed on its purchase	
Artigo Ltd should not charge output tax on the sale of the van because the plumber is not registered for VAT	

(ii) If the accountant at Artigo Ltd is unsure of the correct VAT treatment for the sale of the van, which of the following actions should he take?

Choose **one** answer.

Ask the plumber who is purchasing the van what he believes to be the correct treatment	
Ask the owner of the business, who is not an accountant, whether the business should charge VAT	
Look on the HMRC website for guidance	

(d) **(i)** Artigo Ltd sells goods that are standard-rated for VAT. The net value of the supply made to a customer is £745.24. The customer takes advantage of the prompt payment discount of 2.5% offered by Artigo Ltd.

Calculate the amount of VAT that Artigo Ltd should include in its output VAT for this transaction. Round down to the nearest penny.

£ [   ]

(ii)   Which of the following options are available to Artigo Ltd to account for the VAT on the prompt payment discount the customer has received?

Issue a credit note to the customer for the amount of the PPD, including VAT	
Ignore the VAT on the PPD and include the VAT on the full amount invoiced before discount in the VAT account	
Include a statement on the invoice saying that the customer must ensure it has only recovered the VAT actually paid	
Treat the VAT on the full amount as output tax, and the VAT on the PPD as input VAT	

(e)   Braelife Ltd has made the following expenditure in the last quarter, all of which included VAT at standard rate.

For each of the items of expenditure, identify whether Braelife Ltd can recover the input VAT, or if it is blocked.

	Recover input tax	Input tax blocked
Fuel for the managing director's husband's car		
A staff outing to a local ten pin bowling centre		
A buffet lunch for a presentation to a group of customers in the UK		
Tickets for a rugby match in France for a French customer		

Task 4

This task is about preparing, calculating, and adjusting information for VAT returns.

Karina works for Prestar Ltd as an accounts assistant. Prestar Ltd does not use any of the special VAT accounting schemes.

Karina is currently working on the VAT Return for the quarter ending 30 June.

(a)   Identify which two of the following documents are not relevant when Karina is finalising the VAT Return for the quarter ended 30 June 2023.

Bank statement dated 31 May 2023	
Wages records for April 2023	
Information about a deposit received for an order placed on 20 July 2023	
Credit note received from a supplier dated 14 June 2023	

(b)   At the end of the quarter Karina reviews the VAT Control account. The total value of the debits on the VAT Control Account is £12,431.22 and the value of the credits is £10,424.10. There was no balance brought down on the account at the beginning of the quarter.

Identify which one of the following will be true if Karina now runs the VAT Return using the accounting software.

The business will pay HMRC £2,007.12	
The business will claim a refund from HMRC of £2,007.12	
The business will pay HMRC £10,424.10	
The business will claim a refund from HMRC of £12,431.22	

(c)   **(i)**   Karina has discovered the following genuine error in Prestar Ltd's accounting records which affected the VAT Return for the quarter ending 31 March.

An invoice received from a supplier in March was incorrectly recorded by the accounting software as £1,633.80, including standard-rated VAT. However, the figure should have been £163.38 including VAT.

Calculate the adjustment that should be made to VAT for the quarter. Round your answer down to the nearest penny.

£ [   ]

(ii)   If this is the only error that needs to be adjusted in the VAT quarter ending 30 June 2023, identify the impact on VAT when this error is corrected in the current quarter's VAT Return.

Increase the figure in Box 1	
Decrease the figure in Box 1	
Increase the figure in Box 4	
Decrease the figure in Box 4	

(iii)   Select the correct action for Karina to take in this situation.

Assume that she made an error when she entered the invoice in the accounting software, and take no further action	
Investigate the cause of the error to ensure that there are no issues in the way in which the supplier details have been set up	

(d)   Marina, the owner of the business, has asked Karina to give her £400 from petty cash to pay the decorating company that has repainted the business's meeting rooms. She tells Karina 'There will not be an invoice for this; that way we can all avoid paying any VAT'.

Decide whether the following statements are true or false.

	True	False
Marina is the owner of the business, so Karina must give her the money to pay the decorator		
If Karina gives Marina the cash, she will be compromising her ethical principles		

Task 5

This task is about verifying VAT returns.

Wilma works as the accounts assistant for Luxury Limos Ltd. She is using the business's accounting software to complete the VAT Return for the quarter ended 28 February 2024. The business does not operate any special schemes for VAT. Before calculating the amount due to, or from, HMRC, and submitting the VAT Return, Wilma will need to get approval from the finance manager.

(a) Identify whether each of the following transactions should be included in Box 1 or Box 4 of the VAT Return.

	Box 1	**Box 4**
VAT on a credit note issued to a customer		
VAT on goods taken by a business owner for personal use		
VAT on a sales invoice omitted in error from the previous quarter's VAT return		
VAT on bad debt relief		

(b) The finance manager has asked Wilma to identify the effect of two errors that he has found in the VAT Return for the quarter end 30 November 2023.

Error 1

A purchases invoice for £24,300 plus VAT of £4,860 has been posted twice.

Error 2

VAT on bad debt relief of £2,750 has been added to Box 1 instead of Box 4.

(i) Complete the following statements about the two errors by selecting the correct words.

Error 1: Input tax has been **understated/overstated.**

Error 2: Output tax has been **understated/overstated** and **input tax** has been **understated/overstated.**

(ii) Calculate the value of the net error for the previous quarter. Enter your answer to the nearest penny.

£ [   ]

(iii) Complete the following statement about the effect this will have on the current period's VAT Return about the two errors.

Adjusting for the net error **increases/decreases** the **Box 1/Box 4** figure on the VAT Return for the quarter ended 28 February 2024.

(c) Wilma has established that the net error she has calculated is below the reporting threshold for errors. What action should she now take?

Withdraw the VAT Return for the previous quarter and resubmit it with the correct figures	
Send HMRC a cheque for the net error	
Correct the error on the VAT Return for the quarter ended 28 February 2024	

Task 6

This task is about VAT rules on record keeping, filing and payment/repayment, including non-compliance implications.

(a) Identify whether the following statements about the legal requirements concerning VAT.

	True	False
HMRC can charge interest on VAT that is paid late		
A business that submits its VAT return late can choose whether to pay a £200 penalty or receive late penalty points		
If HMRC makes a mistake that means a business pays too much VAT, it may have to pay interest to the business		
All VAT-registered businesses, including those that register for VAT voluntarily, must comply with Making Tax Digital		

Orscago Ltd has been growing steadily since it was formed 18 months ago. It has now reached the VAT threshold and correctly registered for quarterly VAT accounting. HMRC has confirmed that its first VAT quarter will be for the period to 30 September 2023.

(b) **(i)** What is the latest date that Orscago Ltd can submit its VAT Return for the quarter to 30 September 2023?

(ii) Assuming Orscago Ltd pays its VAT by direct debit, on what date will HMRC collect payment of any VAT due for the quarter to 30 September 2023?

(iii) Because this is the first time that the business has had to submit a VAT Return, the owners of Orscago Ltd did not submit the VAT Return on time.

Identify which of the following will be true in this situation.

Orscago Ltd will have to pay a penalty of £200	
Orscago Ltd will not be penalised as this is its first VAT Return	
Orscago Ltd will receive a late submission penalty point	
Orscago Ltd will receive two late submission penalty points	

(iv) Orscago Ltd holds all its data electronically, including all documents relating to VAT. Identify the final year that Orscago Ltd is required to keep its business records relating to the VAT quarter ended 30 September 2023.

2025	
2027	
2029	
2031	

The owners of Orscago Ltd have been told by another local business owner that it may be beneficial for them to operate the annual accounting scheme for VAT rather than quarterly accounting.

(c)   Identify whether each of the points raised by the owners is true or false.

	True	False
If Orscago Ltd moves to annual accounting for VAT, it will only have to complete one VAT Return per year		
If Orscago Ltd moves to annual accounting for VAT, it will only have to make one VAT payment a year		
Orscago Ltd must have an annual taxable turnover of at least £1.35 million to register for annual accounting for VAT		

Task 7

This task is about the principles of payroll.

(a)   There are a number of documents distributed to employees by their employer.

Match each of the following descriptions with the correct document.

Definition	Payroll document
The form that details expenses and benefits an employee has received in the tax year	
The form that shows the tax an employee has paid on their earnings in the tax year	
Documents given to an employee when they have been paid, detailing the amount of pay, and deductions, including tax and National Insurance Contributions that have been deducted	
The form that the employer gives to an employee who leaves employment with them showing personal and employment data. One part must be given to the individual's new employer	

Payroll documents: P45; P60; P11D; Payslip

(b) Identify whether the following statements about payroll software are true or false.

	True	False
Only businesses that are employers are required to use real time information (RTI) to transmit payroll information to HMRC		
Employers can use a payroll bureau to provide their payroll function if they wish		
Payroll records can be stored electronically, and must be kept for at least three years after the end of the tax year to which they relate		

Myra works as a cleaner for Pristine Places, a local cleaning company. Myra is on a variable hours contract and is paid £12 per hour for the first 25 hours she works each week, and then £15 per hour for any further hours. Myra is enrolled in a work placed pension scheme into which she pays 5% of her salary and Pristine Places pays 3% of her salary.

Pristine Places pays its employees weekly by BACS.

In week 37 Myra worked 31 hours.

(c) **(i)** Complete the table below to calculate Myra's gross pay, pension contributions and the Pristine Places' employer's contribution to Myra's pension.

Week 37	£
Gross Pay	
Employee's pension contribution	
Employer's pension contribution	

(ii) Identify which **two** of the following do not have to be shown on Myra's payslip.

Myra's address	
Myra's National Insurance Contributions for the week	
Myra's net pay for the week	
Details of the bank account that Myra's net pay will be paid into	

Task 8

This task is about reporting information on VAT and payroll.

You are a trainee accountant at Mattsam Ltd, a VAT-registered business that does not operate any of the special accounting schemes. You report to the financial controller.

Today's date is 22 April 2024, and you have just completed the draft VAT Return below.

VAT Return
01 Jan 24 to 31 Mar 24

VAT due on sales and other outputs	1	127451.30
VAT due on intra-community acquisitions of goods made in Northern Ireland from EU Member States	2	zero
Total VAT due (the sum of boxes 1 and 2)	3	127451.30
VAT reclaimed on purchases and other inputs (including acquisitions from the EU)	4	88464.00
Net VAT to be paid to Customs by you (difference between boxes 3 and 4)	5	Calculated value
Total value of sales and all other outputs excluding any VAT	6	678759
Total value of purchases and all other inputs excluding any VAT	7	442320
Total value of intra-community dispatches of goods and related costs, excluding any VAT, from Northern Ireland to EU Member States	8	zero
Total value of intra-community acquisitions of goods and related costs, excluding any VAT, made in Northern Ireland from EU Member States	9	zero

(a) **(i)** Complete the following information that you will include in your email requesting approval of the VAT Return by the financial controller.

The amount due to HMRC is £......	
The date the VAT Return must be submitted by	

(ii) You have received an out of office email from the financial controller which indicates she won't be back in work until you go away on holiday. You are now concerned that the VAT Return may be submitted late if you leave it until you return from your holiday.

Identify what action you should take in this situation.

Submit the VAT Return without the financial controller's approval – any errors can be corrected in the next quarter's VAT Return	
Wait until you are back from your holiday before getting approval	
Ask the owner of the business, Matt Samuels, to approve the VAT Return and authorise the payment	

(b) Mattsam Ltd has just had to write off two large amounts it is owed by customers who have gone into liquidation. It will now have to claim back the VAT on these bad debts. Matt Samuels is concerned about the impact of this on the cash flow of the business.

Identify which of the special accounting schemes would provide automatic relief from bad debt relief.

Annual accounting scheme for VAT	
Cash accounting scheme for VAT	
Flat rate accounting scheme for VAT	

(c) News reports indicate that the Government is considering increasing the standard rate of VAT in the next Budget.

If this occurs, identify whether each of these sentences are true or false about action Mattsam Ltd must take in this situation.

	True	False
It is the responsibility of the accounting software provider to increase the standard VAT on the business's accounting software		
Customers should be informed of the increase in prices caused by the increase in VAT		
The business will not have to amend the rate of VAT it charges until the beginning of the next VAT quarter		
If the business is unsure of what action it should take, it should check the HMRC website		

Practice assessment 2

Task 1

This task is about understanding and calculating UK tax law principles relating to VAT, registration and deregistration, and special schemes.

(a) Identify whether each of the following is classified as a taxable person or not for VAT purposes.

Select **all** options that apply.

	Taxable person	Not a taxable person
A charity with taxable turnover of £110,000		
A business that only makes VAT-exempt supplies		
A business that makes annual sales of £92,250, including reduced rate VAT		

(b) Last year Charlize had a taxable turnover of £98,000; this year her taxable turnover has reduced to £70,000. Decide whether the following statement is true or false.

'Charlize must deregister for VAT immediately.'

TRUE / FALSE

(c) Sarah's turnover for the last year was £105,000. In which of the following circumstances should Sarah immediately register for VAT? Choose **one** option.

All £105,000 is exempt from VAT	
£60,000 is taxable at reduced rate VAT and £45,000 is exempt from VAT	
£60,000 is taxable at standard rate VAT and £45,000 is zero-rated for VAT	

(d) A business reached the VAT registration threshold four months ago but did not realise, and consequently did not register for VAT. Since that date it has invoiced customers £37,500 for standard-rated taxable supplies.

    (i) Decide whether the following sentence is true or false.

        'In this situation the business may be subject to a civil penalty calculated as a percentage of lost revenue.'

        TRUE / FALSE

(ii)   Calculate how much the business must pay to HMRC in respect of output tax for the period that it was not registered.

£ [   ]

(iii)   Decide whether the following sentence is true or false.

'In these circumstances the customers are required to reimburse the business for the VAT that they have paid to HMRC for these sales.'

[TRUE / FALSE]

(e)   Identify which of the following might be a reason for a business to voluntarily register for VAT, even though its taxable turnover is below the VAT registration threshold.

Select **one** option.

The business makes standard-rated supplies, and most of its purchases are zero-rated	
The business makes exempt supplies, and most of its purchases are standard-rated	
The business makes zero-rated supplies and most of its purchases are standard-rated	

Task 2

This task is about calculating and accounting for VAT.

Simone is a trainee accountant at Francis & Brahma and is currently working in the tax department.

Simone is entering some receipts into the accounting software for a client, Cheslie. One receipt is for office stationery. The total amount paid in cash was £127.38, which includes standard rate VAT.

(a)   Identify the VAT and the net amount to be recorded in Cheslie's accounts.

	VAT	Net amount
£21.23		
£25.47		
£106.15		
£127.38		

Simone is unclear when it is compulsory for a VAT-registered business to issue a VAT invoice.

(b) Identify whether a VAT invoice is compulsory, or not compulsory, in each of the following circumstances.

	VAT invoice compulsory	VAT invoice not compulsory
The buyer is not VAT-registered and does not want a VAT invoice		
The buyer is VAT-registered and does not want a VAT invoice		
Where the seller is a retailer, and the customer does not want a VAT invoice		

Simone has been working on the accounts of another client, Dequez Ltd, a business that manages websites for various businesses. Although its customers sign up for the service on an annual basis, Dequez Ltd invoices them on the 1st of every month and collects payment on the 7th.

(c) Identify when a tax point is created for this service.

Once, on the first day of the year to which the contract relates	
Once, on the last day of the year to which the contract relates	
On the 1st of every month when an invoice is issued	
On the 7th of every month when a payment is collected	

Task 3

This task is about the recovery of input tax.

Enderphil Ltd is a VAT-registered business that supplies goods that are a mixture of standard, zero-rated and exempt supplies.

(a)   Which of the following statements is true about input tax the business has incurred?

Choose **one** answer.

All of the input VAT can be reclaimed	
None of the input VAT can be reclaimed	
A restricted amount of the input VAT can be reclaimed, in proportion to the different types of supply	

Enderphil Ltd supplies standard-rated goods to a customer with a net value of £247.14. It gives this customer a trade discount of 1.75%.

(b)   Calculate the amount of VAT to be shown on the invoice that Enderphil Ltd issues to this customer. Round your answer to the nearest penny.

£ [   ]

Enderphil Ltd supplies a standard-rated item to another customer at a price of £785, excluding VAT. The customer pays for the item within 10 days, taking advantage of an 8% prompt payment discount offered by Enderphil Ltd.

(c)   Calculate how much output tax Enderphil Ltd will include in its VAT account for this supply. Round your answer to the nearest penny.

£ [   ]

Merlin has recently set up in business and has already registered for VAT.

Merlin makes the following standard-rated purchases in the first three months of trading. For each of the purchases decide whether the input VAT can be recovered, and if so, how much VAT is recoverable.

(d)   Identify **all** items on which the VAT can be reclaimed and calculate the input VAT that is recoverable.

	Gross amount including VAT £	Input tax recoverable ✔	Input VAT recoverable £
Company delivery van	15,600		
Entertaining prospective customers	522		
Staff party to celebrate a large customer order	330		
New carpet for the staff lounge	144		
New car for Merlin's wife who does one day of secretarial work for the business	11,160		

Ketcherdina Ltd provides a company car for several of its directors and managers.

(e)   **(i)**   Since it was purchased, the business has paid for all the fuel, including VAT at standard rate, for the car provided to the operations manager. The car has CO_2 emissions of 173 g/km.

Identify which of these is the correct fuel scale charge for the VAT quarter ending 31 January 2024.

£1,769	
£459	
£441	
£146	

(ii)   Ketcherdina Ltd leases a car for its sales director. The monthly leasing cost is £628.80, including standard-rated VAT.

Calculate how much of the input VAT on the leasing payment Ketcherdina Ltd can reclaim each month.

£125.76	
£104.80	
£62.88	
£52.40	

(iii)   The owner of Ketcherdina Ltd wants to lease a car for his wife who is not involved in the business. He has told you to treat the car as a business expense and say that it is used by one of the sales team.

How should you respond to this request from the owner?

Do as the owner requests – after all, it is his business	
Report the owner to HMRC immediately	
Explain to the owner that this is not permitted, and to do so would go against your ethical principles	

Task 4

This task is about preparing, calculating, and adjusting information for VAT returns.

Tamsin works for Findera Ltd, a business that submits its VAT Returns on a quarterly basis for the quarters ending 31 January, 30 April, 31 July, and 31 October. The business does not operate any of the special schemes for VAT.

Tamsin is completing the VAT Return for the quarter ended 31 October and has identified two errors that were made in the VAT Return for the quarter ended 31 July.

(a)   For each of the errors below:

  (i)   Calculate the adjustment that needs to be made to VAT. Round your answers down to the nearest penny.

  (ii)   Identify the impact the error will have on VAT (select one of the options from the list below).

	Adjustment £	Impact on VAT (option)
A sales invoice for £200 plus standard rate VAT has been entered as a purchases invoice		
A credit note from a supplier for £223 plus VAT was entered into the accounting software as £2,230 plus VAT		

Options: Increase output tax; decrease output tax; increase input tax; decrease input tax.

(b)   Tamsin has entered an invoice from a new supplier for £425.10 including VAT. The accounting software has calculated the VAT included in the invoice as £20.24. However, the invoice shows the VAT as £70.85.

(i)   Identify the reason for the difference by completing the following statements.

Statement	Options
The invoice from the supplier is	Select from Picklist 1
VAT has been included on the invoice at the	Select from Picklist 2

Picklist 1 options
correct
incorrect

Picklist 2 options
standard rate
reduced rate
zero rate

(ii)   Identify what action Tamsin should take to correct this issue.

Use the figure the accounting software has calculated, and take no further action	
Change the accounting software to ensure the correct rate of VAT is applied to the invoice	
Contact the supplier and explain that the invoice it has sent is incorrect	

(c) Findera Ltd imports standard-rated goods from Spain that it uses in its production process. Tamsin needs to make an adjustment for postponed VAT on imports of £18,270 including VAT made in the quarter.

(i) Decide which of the following statements is correct about this postponed VAT.

VAT of £3,045 must be added to Box 1 of the VAT Return only	
VAT of £3,045 must be added to Box 4 of the VAT Return only	
VAT of £3,045 must be added to Box 1 and Box 4 of the VAT Return	

(ii) Decide whether the following statement is true or false.

'£18,270 needs to be included in Box 7 of the VAT Return.'

TRUE / FALSE

Task 5

This task is about verifying VAT returns.

(a) Identify whether each of the following statements about information included in a VAT Return is true or false.

	True	False
A business must use compatible accounting software for submitting VAT returns under Making Tax Digital (MTD)		
A net error from a previous quarter's VAT Return, that is above the reporting threshold, can be adjusted on the current VAT Return if it is the first time an error adjustment has ever been required		
Exports do not appear in any boxes on a VAT Return as they are zero-rated		
Postponed accounting for VAT on imports is beneficial to the cashflow of a business as it delays payment		

Xantra Ltd has changed accounting software that it uses to calculate VAT. Xantra Ltd operates the cash accounting scheme for VAT.

Niamh, the accounts assistant, has produced the draft VAT Return for the quarter ended 31 August 2023. Niamh's manager has asked her to prepare a reconciliation to the trial balance before the final VAT Return is submitted.

The draft VAT Return for the quarter to 31 August 2023 contains the following figures:

	£
Box 1	17,083.00
Box 4	−9,851.00
Box 5	7,232.00
Box 6	85,415
Box 7	49,255

The VAT liability in the trial balance is £1,786, and Niamh has extracted the figures below from the VAT account in the nominal ledger:

Extract from the trial balance		£
1 June 2023	Brought forward	8.471.40
10 June 2023	Paid to HMRC	−8.471.40
31 August 2023	Output VAT	26,000.00
31 August 2023	Input VAT	13,322.00
31 August 2023	Carried forward	12,678.00

Niamh has also extracted the closing trade receivables figure of £53,502 (including standard rate VAT) and the closing trade payables figure of £20,826 (including standard rate VAT).

(b)   (i)   Identify which of the following is the reason for the difference between the VAT liability figure in the trial balance and the figure on the draft VAT Return.

The draft VAT Return has been incorrectly prepared using normal accounting for VAT	
The VAT Return has been prepared on a cash accounting basis, but the ledger balances include amounts not yet paid or received	
The draft VAT Return has been correctly prepared using normal accounting for VAT	

(ii) Complete the table below to reconcile the figure in the draft VAT Return with the figure in the trial balance. Use a minus sign or brackets where appropriate.

Reconciliation	£
VAT due to HMRC per the draft VAT Return	7,232.00
(Select from Picklist 1)	
(Select from Picklist 2)	
VAT liability per the trial balance	

Picklist 1 options
Output VAT on closing trade receivables
Output VAT on closing trade payables

Picklist 2 options
Input VAT on closing trade receivables
Input VAT on closing trade payables

(c) Because of the issues with reconciling the VAT Return highlighted in part (a), Xantra Ltd submits its VAT Returns for the quarter ending 31 August 2023 late. The business has already submitted three previous VAT Returns late, so has three late submission penalty points.

(i) What will be the late submission penalty because the VAT Return for the quarter ended 31 August 2023 is submitted late?

Select **one** option.

One late submission penalty point	
A penalty of £200	
One late submission penalty point and a penalty of £200	
Four late submission penalty points as this is the fourth late submission	

(ii) If Xantra Ltd submits its VAT Return for the quarter ended 30 November 2023 on time, what will be the effect of this?

Because Xantra Ltd has already reached the late submission penalty point threshold, it will get a penalty of £200.	
Because the VAT Return is on time, one of its late submission penalty points will be removed	
Xantra Ltd will remain at the late submission penalty point threshold of four points but will not get a penalty of £200.	

Task 6

This task is about VAT rules on record keeping, filing and payment/repayment, including non-compliance implications.

Tom is the owner and sole director of Quiscora Ltd, which was incorporated on 1 September 2023. The business has been very busy since that date, and because he has been very busy, Tom was not aware that it actually reached the VAT registration threshold two months ago on 31 January 2024.

(a) **(i)** Identify the maximum percentage of lost revenue that Quiscora Ltd could face as a penalty for late registration.

zero	
30%	
70%	
100%	

(ii) Identify what date HMRC will treat Quiscora Ltd as having been registered for VAT.

1 September 2023	
30 September 2023	
1 March 2024	
1 April 2024	

Tom is currently running Quiscora from his home and is concerned that he does not have sufficient space to store all of the business records that he needs to retain for VAT purposes.

(b) **(i)** Identify which of the following statements is true about the requirements on Quiscora Ltd to maintain VAT records.

	True	**False**
Because space is limited, physical VAT records only need to be kept for two years		
Quiscora Ltd can hold its VAT records electronically		
Business records must be kept for six years after the VAT period to which they relate		

(ii) Identify what the consequence will be of Tom failing to keep business records for the required length of time.

Quiscora Ltd will no longer be able to reclaim VAT on its purchases	
Quiscora Ltd will be issued with a notice of assessment	
Quiscora Ltd will be required to pay a penalty	

Tom is keen to minimise the administration involved in running Quiscora Ltd and has been looking at some of the special schemes for VAT that might be beneficial to the business.

(c) **(i)** Quiscora Ltd has an annual taxable turnover of £124,000 and also makes additional supplies of £37,000 that are exempt from VAT. Decide whether the following statement is true or false.

'Quiscora Ltd is eligible to register for the flat rate scheme.'

TRUE / FALSE

(ii) Identify the discount a business gets on its applicable flat rate for the first 12 months of VAT registration.

0.5%	
1%	
10%	

(iii) Identify which of the following special schemes for VAT a business that is registered under the flat rate scheme for VAT can also register under.

Cash accounting scheme	
Annual accounting scheme	

Task 7

This task is about the principles of payroll.

(a) Match each of the definitions in the table below with the correct payroll term.

Definition	Options
The system for calculating and applying deductions for Income Tax	
The amount of untaxed, or free, pay that an employee is entitled to in one year	
Amounts paid to the government by employers and employees to fund benefits for people who are retired, sick or unemployed	
The online process for submitting payroll information to HMRC	

Options
Real Time Information (RTI)
Pay As You Earn (PAYE)
Personal allowance
National Insurance Contributions

Greta is an accounts assistant at Greener World. The business uses a payroll bureau to process its payroll. She is keen to understand more about the payroll process.

(b) **(i)** Identify whether each of the following statements about payroll deductions is true or false.

	True	False
National Insurance Contributions are only made by employees		
Student loan repayments are a statutory payroll deduction that is made once an employee's earnings exceed a defined threshold		
Union membership fees are a statutory deduction		
An employer is required to offer employees over the age of 22 a workplace pension, and must make contributions if the employee earns above a specified amount		

(ii) Greta is required to distribute various payroll forms to the employees of Greener World.

Complete the table below to show the dates by which each payroll form should be distributed to the staff at Greener World for the tax year 2023/24.

Form	Required distribution date
P60	
P11D	

(iii) The business has just taken on three new employees. Greta needs to understand two of the forms that are relevant to processing the new employees for payroll.

Form	Options
The form that an employee will have received from their previous employee, summarising information about their employment and pay to date	(Select from Picklist 1)
The form that is submitted to HMRC detailing payments to employees, deductions made, and details of new employees and employees that leave	(Select from Picklist 2)

Picklist 1 options
P11D
Payslip
P45

Picklist 2 options
Full Payment Submission (FPS)
Employer Payment Summary (EPS)
Employment allowance

Task 8

This task is about reporting information on VAT and payroll.

Francis works as the accounts assistant for Inkpen Ltd, a small stationery wholesaler. One of his roles is to prepare the monthly payroll.

The warehouse supervisor approves all hours worked by the warehouse staff.

Payment to staff is made by BACS by the business owner, Stella.

Inkpen Ltd uses an external firm of accountants to prepare its year-end accounts.

Francis has completed the wages report for February 2024 and extracted the following information:

	£
Gross wages	28,464.56
Income Tax	3,142.50
Employers' NIC	1,113.01
Employees' NIC	1,547.25
Employer's Pension Contributions	1,138.58
Employees' Pension Contributions	11,992.52
Student loan deductions	94.34

(a) **(i)** Identify who should approve the wages report.

The warehouse supervisor	
Stella	
Francis	
The external accountant	

(ii) Decide whether the following statement is true or false.

'The external accountant will not require the wages report to complete the year-end accounts as all the information will be included in the trial balance.'

TRUE / FALSE

(iii) Complete the following sentences about the payroll information.

The amount due to HMRC is ……	£
The date this amount must be paid to HMRC by is …..	

One of the employees at Inkpen Ltd is currently on an apprenticeship which involves him attending the local college one day per week. He has told Francis that his college class was told that the minimum hourly rate for apprentices is to be increased from April 2024.

(b)   Identify which **two** sources would provide Francis with the correct information about the possible increase in the pay rate for apprentices.

The local college	
The gov.uk website	
Stella, the owner of the business	
Update from the payroll software provider used by Inkpen Ltd	
An article in a national newspaper	

The external accountant has suggested to Francis that Inkpen Ltd may be eligible for employment allowance.

(c)   Identify which **two** of these statements are true about employment allowance.

The maximum reduction in Class 1 NIC an employer can get if it is eligible for employment allowance is £5,000	
Any business that claims employment allowance only needs to make quarterly payroll payments to HMRC	
A business may be eligible for employment allowance if its National Insurance Contributions do not exceed £100,000	
Employment allowance should be claimed on the employer's Full Payment Submission (FPS)	

Practice
assessment 3

Task 1

This task is about understanding and calculating UK tax law principles relating to VAT, registration and deregistration, and special schemes.

(a)   Complete the following statement by selecting **one** option.

Voluntary registration for VAT is available for any business …

… that has been trading for more than three years	
… that makes at least some taxable supplies	
… with taxable turnover greater than the VAT registration threshold	

(b)   A business that is not currently registered for VAT makes only standard-rated supplies. Its sales over the last 12 months have stayed at a steady average of £6,000 a month. On 1 August the business accepts an order for £81,000 of goods to be delivered and invoiced at the end of August. The customer will be expected to pay for the goods within 30 days of receipt of the invoice.

Identify the statement that best describes the requirement on the business to register for VAT On 1 August.

The business is not yet required to register as its taxable turnover for the past 12 months is below the VAT registration threshold	
The business must register without delay because the new order plus the average month's sales is for an amount in excess of the VAT registration threshold	
The business will exceed the VAT registration threshold in the 12 month period to 31 August and must register on 31 August	

Halliways Ltd started trading on 1 May 2023. The business sells a mixture of standard-rated and zero-rated goods. Sales for the first five months of trading are shown in the table below.

(c) **(i)** Complete the table to show the monthly taxable supplies for Halliways Ltd and the cumulative taxable supplies for the months May 2023 to September 2023.

Show your answers to the nearest whole pound (£).

Month	Standard rate supplies £	Zero rate supplies £	Monthly taxable supplies £	Cumulative taxable supplies £
May 2023	17,700	7,450	25,150	25,150
June 2023	18,900	6,900	25,800	50,950
July 2023	16,200	9,700	25,900	76,850
August 2023	17,200	5,400	22,600	99,450
September 2023	17,750	3,100	20,850	120,300

Note: in the AAT assessment, the system will autofill some of the calculated figures for this answer.

(ii) Identify the month end on which Halliways Ltd will exceed the VAT registration threshold.

> 31 August 2023

(iii) Under the historic turnover method, identify the month end date by which Halliways Ltd must register for VAT.

> 30 September 2023

A VAT-registered business operates a single special accounting scheme for VAT and has the following characteristics:

- the business has a taxable turnover of £750,000 per year
- the business only pays output tax to HMRC when it has been received from its customers
- the business only reclaims input tax from HMRC when it has been paid to its suppliers
- the business cannot claim bad debt relief

(d) Identify which special scheme this business is operating.

The cash accounting scheme	✓
The annual accounting scheme	
The flat rate scheme	

(e) A bookkeeper that uses the flat rate scheme for VAT, but that is classified as a limited cost business, must use which of the following flat rates?

5%	
14.5%	
16.5%	
20%	

Task 2

This task is about calculating and accounting for VAT.

Bromsing Ltd is a VAT-registered business that sells a variety of standard-rated and zero-rated items.

Vanessa has extracted the draft VAT Return for the business for the quarter ended 30 September 2023 from the accounting software.

The figure in Box 3 is £35,380 and the figure in Box 4 is £49,726.

(a) **(i)** Identify the action that Vanessa will now have to take.

Vanessa will have to arrange payment to HMRC of £14,346	
Vanessa will have to reclaim £14,346 from HMRC	
Vanessa will have to arrange payment to HMRC of £35,380	
Vanessa will have to reclaim £49,726 from HMRC	

Bromsing Ltd wishes to issue simplified invoices.

(ii) Identify which of the following statements is true about simplified invoices.

Bromsing Ltd can issue a simplified invoice for standard-rated items of £215 plus VAT	
Bromsing Ltd can issue a simplified invoice for a mixed supply of zero-rated items of £80 and standard-rated items of £150 plus VAT	
Bromsing Ltd can issue a simplified invoice for a mixed supply of standard-rated items of £140 including VAT and zero-rated items of £100	

(iii) Identify which one of the following items of information can be omitted from a simplified invoice.

The tax point	
The seller's VAT registration number	
The seller's address	
The amount of VAT	
A description of the goods and services	

(b) A business delivers goods to a customer on 15 May and issues a VAT invoice on 21 May.

Identify the tax point for this supply.

1 May	
15 May	
21 May	
31 May	

(c) A VAT-registered business that sells health products supplies a trade customer with the following items:

- Zero-rated items for £375

- Standard-rated items for £893 plus VAT

A trade discount of 3% is offered.

Identify how much VAT should be included on the invoice.

£245.99	
£178.60	
£173.24	
£75.00	

(d) A business supplies a standard-rated item at a price of £788 excluding VAT. The customer is entitled to a 5% trade discount and pays for the item within 10 days which allows it to take advantage of an 8% prompt payment discount offered by the business.

Calculate how much output tax should be included in the business's VAT account for this supply.

£ [   ]

(e) Calculate the missing figures in the table below to show VAT at the standard rate on net and gross amounts.

Round your answer to the nearest penny.

Net £	VAT £	Gross £
247.20		
		341.22

Task 3

This task is about the recovery of input tax.

(a) Identify which of the following describes residual input tax.

VAT incurred on costs and expenses that have been paid for before the due date in order to obtain prompt payment discount	
VAT incurred on costs and expenses that have not been paid for at the end of the VAT accounting period	
VAT incurred on costs and expenses that cannot definitely be attributed to taxable supplies or to exempt supplies	
VAT incurred on costs and expenses that can definitely be attributed to taxable supplies or to zero-rated supplies	

Alkadi Ltd is a VAT-registered business that supplies taxable and exempt products. Julius, the finance assistant, is keen to understand how this affects the input VAT that the business incurs.

(b) Decide whether each of the following statements is true or false.

	True	False
A business with average total input tax per month of £1,500, including exempt input tax of £600, can claim back all its input VAT		
A business can claim back all input VAT if its exempt input tax is 20%, or less, of its total input tax		

Alkadi Ltd has incurred the following expenses in the VAT quarter.

Alkadi has purchased four laptops at a total of £4,800 plus VAT that will be used by the sales team. The team has been told that they can use them at the weekend and in the evenings for personal use.

(c) **(i)** Identify whether the input tax on each of the following items is recoverable, partly recoverable, or blocked.

	Input tax recoverable	Input tax partly recoverable	Input tax blocked
The cost of the tickets for staff to attend an awards ceremony where Alkadi Ltd won an award			
A business dinner with three members of staff from a prospective customer, attended by the sales manager and two of the sales team			
Centre court tickets at Wimbledon for a customer as a thank you for its business			

(ii) Julius has estimated that, on average, the laptops will be used 25% of the time for personal use.

Calculated how much of the VAT on the laptops can be treated as input tax in Alkadi Ltd's VAT return.

£ _____

The credit controller left Alkadi Ltd eight months ago and since then, the business has struggled to collect its debts. Julius has carried out a detailed review of the aged receivables at the end of the financial year to 28 February 2024 and has identified several bad debts.

(d) For each bad debt Julius has identified:

(i) Identify whether bad debt relief can be claimed

(ii) Calculate the amount of bad debt relief available. Round figures down to the nearest penny.

Bad debt	Eligible for bad debt relief	Not eligible for bad debt relief	Amount of bad debt relief available £
Charles and Co was invoiced on 1 June 2023 for £2,340. It paid £1,422, but is disputing the remainder. The balance has been written off in the accounts of Alkadi Ltd			
Manuka Ltd owes a total of £2,745. Alkadi Ltd has not traded with Manuka Ltd for 12 months, and has set up a bad debt provision for 80% of the outstanding amount			

(e) Alina operates as a sole trader. She has a car which she uses 60% for the business and 40% for personal use. It has CO_2 emissions of 163 g/km. In the quarter ended 28 February 2024, the business has paid £960 including VAT, for fuel for Alina's car.

Alina's business reclaims all of the VAT on the fuel and uses the appropriate fuel scale charge to account for Alina's private use.

Identify the correct VAT on the fuel scale charge for the quarter ended 28 February 2024.

£270.33	
£134.00	
£70.50	
£67.50	

Task 4

This task is about preparing, calculating, and adjusting information for VAT returns.

Rachel is an assistant accountant at Johns & Co, a firm of accountants. She is currently working on the VAT Return for Homilies Ltd for the quarter ended 30 June 2023.

Homilies Ltd operates the cash accounting scheme for VAT.

Rachel has reviewed the bank reconciliation for the quarter ended 31 March 2023 and identified that four transactions have been omitted from the accounting software.

(a) Calculate the changes that need to be made to the figures for output and input tax for each transaction. Round your answer down to the nearest penny. If there is no change enter 0.00.

Transaction	Change to input tax £	Change to output tax £
10 January 2023 £324, direct debit payment for the business's quarterly internet and telephone supply, on which standard rate VAT has been charged		
24 January 2023 £3,360, cash from the sale of a business van. Homilies Ltd claimed input VAT on the original purchase of the van		
12 February 2023 £4,123.98 paid to HMRC for VAT for the quarter ended 31 December 2020		
1 March 2023 £196.35, payment from a customer for goods on which Homilies Ltd charges reduced rate VAT		

The owner of Homilies Ltd is considering switching suppliers to a business located in Switzerland. He has asked Rachel some questions about the implications of importing raw materials.

(b) Identify whether each of the following statements is true or false.

	True	False
VAT on imports to the UK is normally charged at the same rate as if it had been supplied in the UK		
If a VAT-registered business is using postponed VAT accounting, this means the payment of VAT is speeded up		
VAT on imports accounted for through postponed VAT accounting is included in the Box 1 and Box 4 figures on the VAT Return		

(c) Identify which of the following trading conditions would result in a business regularly receiving a refund from HMRC.

The business makes standard-rated supplies and purchases zero-rated goods and services	
The business makes exempt supplies and purchases standard-rated goods and services	
The business makes zero-rated supplies and purchases standard-rated goods and services	
The business makes exempt supplies and purchases zero-rated goods and services	

Task 5

This task is about verifying VAT returns.

Jonas is the assistant account for Growlerly Ltd. He has been asked to prepare the VAT return for the quarter ended 30 April 2023.

The standard rate of VAT is 20%.

The following accounts have been extracted from the accounting software:

Purchases account

Date 2023	Reference	Debit £	Date 2023	Reference	Credit £
01/02 -30/04	Purchases daybook – UK purchases	328,091.50	30/04	Balance c/d	356,181.86
01/02 -30/04	Purchases daybook – zero-rated purchases	28,090.36			
	Total	356,181.86		Total	356,181.86

VAT account

Date 2023	Reference	Debit £	Date 2023	Reference	Credit £
01/02 -30/04	Purchases daybook – UK purchases	65,618.30	01/02 -30/04	Sales daybook – UK sales	30,705.57
			01/02 -30/04	Cash book – UK sales	2,057.17

You are told that UK purchases included a delivery van for £27,750 plus VAT, and a company car for the Sales Director which he will use for business and private use for £36,250 plus VAT. The related VAT for both purchases is included in the VAT account figure.

(a) **(i)** Calculate the correct Box 1 figure for the VAT Return.

£ [   ]

(ii) Calculate the correct Box 4 figure for the VAT Return.

£ [   ]

(iii) Calculate the correct Box 5 figure for the VAT Return. If the figure is a refund use a minus sign.

£ [   ]

Jonas has just discovered the following two non-deliberate, careless errors that were made on the previous VAT Return:

Error 1   VAT of £121 on a purchases invoice from a UK supplier was entered twice in the accounting software.

Error 2   A credit note received from a UK supplier for £444, including standard rate VAT, was not recorded in the accounting software.

The business is permitted to correct the net error on the current VAT Return.

(b)   **(i)**   Complete the following statements about the two errors by selecting the correct words:

Error 1 has resulted in **input / output** tax being **understated / overstated.**

Error 2 has resulted in **input / output** tax being **understated / overstated.**

(ii)   Calculate the value of the net error for the previous quarter. Enter your answer to the nearest penny.

£ [   ]

(iii)   Identify which of the following corrections Jonas should make on the VAT Return for the current quarter.

Add £195 to Box 1	
Add £47 to Box 1	
Deduct £195 from Box 4	
Deduct £47 from Box 4	

The Box 6 figure on Growlerly Ltd's VAT Return for the previous quarter was £201,460.

(c)   Identify the reporting threshold for error in the previous quarter's VAT Return for Growlerly Ltd.

£20,146	
£10,000	
£2,014.60	
£201.46	

It is now two weeks after Jonas submitted the VAT Return for the quarter ended 30 April 2023. He has realised that there was a large error in the figures that he had not identified, which will result in the business having to pay HMRC a significant additional amount of VAT.

Jonas is concerned about losing his job if he raises the issue with his manager but is also aware that the business may incur a misdeclaration penalty if it fails to report it to HMRC.

(d) Identify the ethical course of action that Jonas should take in this situation.

Do not tell anyone and hope that the error is not discovered	
Correct the error on the next VAT Return despite knowing that it should be separately disclosed	
Explain to the Finance Manager that he has made the error and that the business must make a voluntary disclosure of the error	
Contact HMRC himself, and make a voluntary disclosure of the error	

Task 6

This task is about VAT rules on record keeping, filing and payment/repayment, including non-compliance implications.

(a) **(i)** Identify whether each of the following statements about the legal requirements relating to VAT is true or false.

	True	False
A default penalty of £200 is charged by HMRC if a business decides to deregister for VAT		
If a business fails to submit a VAT Return on time, HMRC can issue a VAT notice of assessment that estimates the amount of VAT due		
Any late submission penalty points a business has automatically expire after a year		
HMRC cannot charge interest if a business does not report and pay the correct amount of VAT		

(ii) Complete the following sentence by inserting the correct number.

'The rate of interest that HMRC can charge on VAT that is late is calculated as the Bank of England base rate plus

%.'

Rice Ltd is VAT-registered on the annual accounting scheme for VAT, with an annual accounting period that ends on 31 December each year. Its VAT liability for the annual VAT period ended 31 December 2023 was £174,300.

Rice Ltd has elected to make three interim payments.

(b) **(i)** Identify which months in 2023 Rice Ltd will make its three interim payments of VAT to HMRC for the annual accounting period that ends 31 December 2023.

January, May, September	
February, May, August	
March, July, November	
April, July, October	

(ii) Calculate how much each of the three interim payments must be.

£ [   ]

(iii) Identify the date by which Rice Ltd must submit its VAT Return for the annual accounting period and pay the balance due.

31 December 2023	
31 January 2024	
10 February 2024	
28 February 2024	

(c) Most businesses now pay their VAT liability electronically.

Identify whether each of the following statements is true or false.

	True	False
If VAT is due to HMRC, it will collect three days after the date that the VAT Return is due		
If a repayment of VAT is due to a business, HMRC will make the payment three days after the date on which the VAT Return is due		

Task 7

This task is about the principles of payroll.

(a) Identify the documents on which each of the following must be included.

Information	P60	P11D	Payslip
The amount of tax an employee has paid on their earnings in the tax year			
The gross amount of pay in a pay period before any deductions			
Details of a company car provided to an employee			
Private medical insurance paid for by an employer for an employee			
The number of hours worked by an employee on a variable hours contract			

Dexter joined Borders Ltd on 1 June 2023. He has queried the figures on his P60 from the 2023/24 tax year as it shows a higher figure than he actually received in the year which was a total of £20,697.43.

His P60 shows the following information:

Pay and Income Tax details		£
	Pay £	**Tax deducted** £
In previous employment(s)	4,812.20	543.50
In this employment	25,944.20	3,090.10
Total for the year	30,756.40	3,633.60

Employee's National Insurance in this employment	2,156.67

(b) Complete the reconciliation below to explain to Dexter why the amount he has received differs from the amount on his P60 for 2023/24.

	£
Amounts received	20,697.43
(Select from Picklist)	
(Select from Picklist)	
Amount per P60 in 2021/22	

Picklist options
PAYE
Employees' National Insurance Contributions
Employers' National Insurance Contributions
Net Pay

Border Ltd has failed to file its Full Payment Submission (FPS) on time for the second time in the 2023/24 tax year. The business employs 37 full-time staff and 16 part-time staff.

(c) **(i)** Identify what the penalty will be for this.

£100	
£200	
£300	
£500	

(ii) Complete the following statement about maintaining payroll records.

'An employer must keep payroll records for a minimum of [   ] years after the end of

the tax year to which they relate. Failure to do so may result in a penalty of £ [   ] .

Task 8

This task is about reporting information on VAT and payroll.

You are an assistant accountant who works for Fabulous Feasts, a restaurant group with a number of locations across the country. You have been asked to draft an email advising the owner of the business how a decrease in the rate of VAT would affect their restaurants, and what action they need to take as a consequence.

(a) Complete the following text for the draft email by selecting the correct words to complete the sentences.

Sentence	Options
As the VAT rate is decreasing the business must consider whether the menu prices charged to customers, which are inclusive of VAT, should change. These prices......	Select from Picklist 1
The new rate of VAT must be reflected in the amount of VAT we pay to HMRC......	Select from Picklist 2
If the date of the change in VAT rate falls during one of our VAT periods, our system must......	Select from Picklist 3

Picklist 1
...cannot change until the date of the next VAT Return.
...must change on the date of the VAT change.
...can remain unchanged if the business chooses.

Picklist 2
...only if we change the prices to customers.
...whether we change the prices to customers or not.
...only if customers choose to pay the new prices.

Picklist 3
...apply a single rate of VAT during that VAT period.
...apply both the old and the new rates of VAT during that VAT period, depending on the size of the customer's bill.
...apply both the old and the new rates of VAT during that VAT period, depending on the date of each meal.

You have recently been trained on how to use the accounting software at Fabulous Feasts, to prepare the quarterly VAT Returns.

(b) Identify which two of the following events would prompt you to check whether the accounting software needed to be updated:

You have received an email from the software provider saying the software licence needs to be renewed	
One of the restaurant managers suggested that all computer software needs to be updated every two months	
You receive an email from HMRC about a change in the way in which VAT Returns are submitted	
When you log on to the accounting software there is a notification stating that an update is required	

You are aware that it is important for you to maintain up-to-date and relevant knowledge about VAT.

(c) **(i)** Identify which **two** of these options would help to ensure this.

Ensure that the license for the accounting software is renewed annually	
Attending relevant Continuing Professional Development provided by AAT	
Having quarterly meetings with the owner of the busines to explain the content of the VAT Return	
Subscribe to the HMRC email updates on VAT and ensure you read them regularly	

(ii) Identify which fundamental ethical principles set out in the AAT Code of Professional Ethics you are adhering to if you do maintain this knowledge.

Integrity	
Confidentiality	
Professional competence and due care	
Professional behaviour	

Answers to practice assessment 1

Task 1

(a)

HMRC is the tax authority for all taxes in the UK	✔
Businesses that only import goods from abroad are not regulated by HMRC	
HMRC will normally give businesses seven days' notice before a VAT visit	✔
HMRC is independent of the UK Government	

(b)

The business will not have to register for VAT in the next year but can do so voluntarily	✔
The business will not be eligible to register for VAT at any point in the next year	
The business will be required to register for VAT at some point in the next year	

(c)

Flat rate scheme	
Cash accounting scheme	
Annual accounting scheme	✔

(d)

... almost immediately	✔
... within the next six months	
… within the next 12 months	

(e)

A business makes supplies of £120 including VAT of £20	Standard rate
A business makes supplies of £225 on which no VAT can be charged	Exempt
A business makes supplies of £145 plus VAT of £7.25	Reduced rate
A business sends an invoice to a customer for £324.50 which states that the VAT is £nil	Zero rate

Task 2

(a)   FALSE. A simplified invoice can only be issued if the total amount, including VAT, is less than £250. Here, £224 plus 20% VAT is £268.80

(b)

	Net	VAT	Gross
	£	£	£
Four car seat covers (standard rate VAT)	197.20	39.44	236.64
Children's travel system (reduced rate VAT)	430.00	21.50	451.50
DAB radio (standard rate)	234.00	46.80	280.80

(c)

The tax point for the deposit is 25 January and for the balance is 28 January	✔
The tax point for the deposit is 26 January and for the balance is 1 February	
The tax point for the deposit and the balance is 26 January	
The tax point for the deposit and the balance is 28 January	

(d)   17 September

Task 3

(a)

If the exempt supplies exceed the 'de minimis' limit, all of the input tax can be reclaimed	
If the zero-rated supplies exceed the 'de minimis' limit, all of the input tax can be reclaimed	
If the exempt supplies are below the 'de minimis' limit, all of the input tax can be reclaimed	✔
If the zero-rated supplies are below the 'de minimis' limit, all of the input tax can be reclaimed	

(b) **(i)** £390

(ii)

In its VAT period ending 28 February	
In its VAT period ending 31 May	
In its VAT period ending 31 August	
In its VAT period ending 30 November	✔

(c) **(i)**

Artigo Ltd should charge output tax on the sale of the van because the plumber is going to use it solely for business purposes	
Artigo Ltd should charge output tax on the sale of the van because input VAT was claimed on its purchase	✔
Artigo Ltd should not charge output tax on the sale of the van because the plumber is not registered for VAT	

(ii)

Ask the plumber who is purchasing the van what he believes to be the correct treatment	
Ask the owner of the business, who is not an accountant, whether the business should charge VAT	
Look on the HMRC website for guidance	✔

(d) **(i)** £145.32

(ii)

Issue a credit note to the customer for the amount of the PPD, including VAT	✔
Ignore the VAT on the PPD and include the VAT on the full amount invoiced before discount in the VAT account	
Include a statement on the invoice saying that the customer must ensure it has only recovered the VAT actually paid	✔
Treat the VAT on the full amount as output tax, and the VAT on the PPD as input VAT	

(e)

	Recover input tax	Input tax blocked
Fuel for the managing director's husband's car		✔
A staff outing to a local ten pin bowling centre	✔	
A buffet lunch for a presentation to a group of customers in the UK		✔
Tickets for a rugby match in France for a French customer	✔	

Task 4

(a)

Bank statement dated 31 May 2023	
Wages records for April 2023	✔
Information about a deposit received for an order placed on 20 July 2023	✔
Credit note received from a supplier 14 June 2023	

(b)

The business will pay HMRC £2,007.12	
The business will claim a refund from HMRC of £2,007.12	✔
The business will pay HMRC £10,424.10	
The business will claim a refund from HMRC of £12,431.22	

(c)   **(i)**   £245.07

Working: (£1,633.80 x 1/6) – (£163.38 x 1/6) = £245.07

(ii)

Increase the figure in Box 1	✔
Decrease the figure in Box 1	
Increase the figure in Box 4	
Decrease the figure in Box 4	

(iii)

Assume that she made an error when she entered the invoice in the accounting software, and take no further action	
Investigate the cause of the error to ensure that there are no issues in the way in which the supplier details have been set up	✔

(d)

	True	False
Marina is the owner of the business, so Karina must give her the money to pay the decorator		✔
If Karina gives Marina the cash, she will be compromising her ethical principles	✔	

Task 5

(a)

	Box 1	Box 4
VAT on a credit note issued to a customer	✔	
VAT on goods taken by a business owner for personal use	✔	
VAT on a sales invoice omitted in error from the previous quarter's VAT return	✔	
VAT on bad debt relief		✔

(b) **(i)** Error 1: Input tax has been **overstated.**

Error 2: Output tax has been **overstated** and **input tax** has been **understated.**

(ii) £640

(iii) Adjusting for the net error **increases** the **Box 4** figure on the VAT Return for the quarter ended 28 February 2024.

(c)

Withdraw the VAT Return for the previous quarter and resubmit it with the correct figures	
Send HMRC a cheque for the net error	
Correct the error on the VAT Return for the quarter ended 28 February 2024	✔

Task 6

(a)

	True	False
HMRC can charge interest on VAT that is paid late	✔	
A business that submits its VAT return late can choose whether to pay a £200 penalty or receive late penalty points		✔
If HMRC makes a mistake that means a business pays too much VAT, it may have to pay interest to the business	✔	
All VAT-registered businesses, including those that register for VAT voluntarily, must comply with Making Tax Digital	✔	

(b) **(i)** 7 November 2023

(ii) 10 November 2023

(iii)

Orscago Ltd will have to pay a penalty of £200	
Orscago Ltd will not be penalised as this is its first VAT Return	✔
Orscago Ltd will receive a late submission penalty point	
Orscago Ltd will receive two late submission penalty points	

(iv)

2025	
2027	
2029	✔
2031	

(c)

	True	False
If Orscago Ltd moves to annual accounting for VAT, it will only have to complete one VAT Return per year	✔	
If Orscago Ltd moves to annual accounting for VAT, it will only have to make one VAT payment a year		✔
Orscago Ltd must have an annual taxable turnover of at least £1.35 million to register for annual accounting for VAT		✔

Task 7

(a)

Definition	Payroll document
The form that details expenses and benefits an employee has received in the tax year	P11D
The form that shows the tax an employee has paid on their earnings in the tax year	P60
Documents given to an employee when they have been paid, detailing the amount of pay, and deductions, including tax and National Insurance Contributions that have been deducted	Payslip
The form that the employer gives to an employee who leaves employment with them showing personal and employment data. One part must be given to the individual's new employer	P45

(b)

	True	False
Only businesses that are employers are required to use real time information (RTI) to transmit payroll information to HMRC		✔
Employers can use a payroll bureau to provide their payroll function if they wish	✔	
Payroll records can be stored electronically, and must be kept for at least three years after the end of the tax year to which they relate	✔	

(c) **(i)**

Week 37	£
Gross Pay	390.00
Employee's pension contribution	19.50
Employer's pension contribution	11.70

(ii)

Myra's address	✔
Myra's National Insurance Contributions for the week	
Myra's net pay for the week	
Details of the bank account that Myra's net pay will be paid into	✔

Task 8

(a) **(i)**

The amount due to HMRC is £......	38,987.30
The date the VAT Return must be submitted by	7 May 2024

(ii)

Submit the VAT Return without the financial controller's approval – any errors can be corrected in the next quarter's VAT Return	
Wait until you are back from your holiday before getting approval	
Ask the owner of the business, Matt Samuels, to approve the VAT Return and authorise the payment	✔

(b)

Annual accounting scheme for VAT	
Cash accounting scheme for VAT	✔
Flat rate accounting scheme for VAT	

(c)

	True	False
It is the responsibility of the accounting software provider to increase the standard VAT on the business's accounting software		✔
Customers should be informed of the increase in prices caused by the increase in VAT	✔	
The business will not have to amend the rate of VAT it charges until the beginning of the next VAT quarter		✔
If the business is unsure of what action it should take, it should check the HMRC website	✔	

Answers to practice assessment 2

Task 1

(a)

	Taxable person	Not a taxable person
A charity with taxable turnover of £110,000	✔	
A business that only makes VAT-exempt supplies		✔
A business that makes annual sales of £92,250, including reduced rate VAT	✔	

(b) FALSE. Although her turnover has fallen below the deregistration threshold, Charlize can choose whether to remain VAT-registered or not.

(c)

All £105,000 is exempt from VAT	
£60,000 is taxable at reduced rate VAT and £45,000 is exempt from VAT	
£60,000 is taxable at standard rate VAT and £45,000 is zero-rated for VAT	✔

(d) **(i)** TRUE. Although the business did not deliberately fail to register for VAT, it may still be subject to a penalty which could be up to 30% of potential lost revenue.

(ii) £6,250

Working: £37,500 x 1/6

(iii) FALSE. The business can attempt to recover the VAT from its customers, but they have no obligation to pay it.

(e)

The business makes standard-rated supplies, and most of its purchases are zero-rated	
The business makes exempt supplies, and most of its purchases are standard-rated	
The business makes zero-rated supplies and most of its purchases are standard-rated	✔

Task 2

(a)

	VAT	Net amount
£21.23	✔	
£25.47		
£106.15		✔
£127.38		

(b)

	VAT invoice compulsory	VAT invoice not compulsory
The buyer is not VAT-registered and does not want a VAT invoice		✔
The buyer is VAT-registered and does not want a VAT invoice	✔	
Where the seller is a retailer, and the customer does not want a VAT invoice		✔

(c)

Once, on the first day of the year to which the contract relates	
Once, on the last day of the year to which the contract relates	
On the 1st of every month when an invoice is issued	✔
On the 7th of every month when a payment is collected	

Task 3

(a)

All of the input VAT can be reclaimed	
None of the input VAT can be reclaimed	
A restricted amount of the input VAT can be reclaimed, in proportion to the different types of supply	✔

(b)   £48.56

(c) £144.44

(d)

	Gross amount including VAT £	Input tax recoverable ✔	Input VAT recoverable £
Company delivery van	15,600	✔	2,600
Entertaining prospective customers	522		
Staff party to celebrate a large customer order	330	✔	55
New carpet for the staff lounge	144	✔	24
New car for Merlin's wife who does one day of secretarial work for the business	11,160		

(e)   **(i)**

£1,769	
£459	
£441	✔
£146	

(ii)

£125.76	
£104.80	
£62.88	
£52.40	✔

(iii)

Do as the owner requests – after all, it is his business	
Report the owner to HMRC immediately	
Explain to the owner that this is not permitted, and to do so would go against your ethical principles	✔

Task 4

(a)

	Adjustment £	Impact on VAT
A sales invoice for £200 plus standard rate VAT has been entered as a purchases invoice	80	Increase output tax
A credit note from a supplier for £223 plus VAT was entered into the accounting software as £2,230 plus VAT	401.40	Increase input tax

(b) **(i)**

Statement	Options
The invoice from the supplier is	correct
VAT has been included on the invoice at the ...	standard rate

(i)

Use the figure the accounting software has calculated, and take no further action	
Change the accounting software to ensure the correct rate of VAT is applied to the invoice	✔
Contact the supplier and explain that the invoice it has sent is incorrect	

(c) **(i)**

VAT of £3,045 must be added to Box 1 of the VAT Return only	
VAT of £3,045 must be added to Box 4 of the VAT Return only	
VAT of £3,045 must be added to Box 1 and Box 4 of the VAT Return	✔

(ii) FALSE. The net amount of £15,225 should be included in Box 7 of the VAT Return.

Task 5

(a)

	True	False
A business must use compatible accounting software for submitting VAT returns under Making Tax Digital (MTD)	✔	
A net error from a previous quarter's VAT Return, that is above the reporting threshold, can be adjusted on the current VAT Return if it is the first time an error adjustment has ever been required		✔
Exports do not appear in any boxes on a VAT Return as they are zero-rated		✔
Postponed accounting for VAT on imports is beneficial to the cashflow of a business as it delays payment	✔	

(b)   **(i)**

The draft VAT Return has been incorrectly prepared using normal accounting for VAT	
The VAT Return has been prepared on a cash accounting basis, but the ledger balances include amounts not yet paid or received	✔
The draft VAT Return has been correctly prepared using normal accounting for VAT	

(ii)

Reconciliation	£
VAT due to HMRC per the draft VAT Return	7,232.00
Output VAT on closing trade receivables	8.917.00
Input VAT on closing trade payables	–3.471.00
VAT liability per the trial balance	12,678.00

(c) **(i)**

One late submission penalty point	
A penalty of £200	
One late submission penalty point and a penalty of £200	✔
Four late submission penalty points as this is the fourth late submission	

(ii)

Because Xantra Ltd has already reached the late submission penalty point threshold, it will get a penalty of £200.	
Because the VAT Return is on time, one of its late submission penalty points will be removed	
Xantra Ltd will remain at the late submission penalty point threshold of four points but will not get a penalty of £200.	✔

Task 6

(a) **(i)**

zero	
30%	✔
70%	
100%	

(ii) Identify what date HMRC will treat Quiscora Ltd as having been registered for VAT.

1 September 2023	
30 September 2023	
1 March 2024	✔
! April 2024	

(b) **(i)**

	True	False
Because space is limited, physical VAT records only need to be kept for two years		✔
Quiscora Ltd can hold its VAT records electronically	✔	
Business records must be kept for six years after the VAT period to which they relate	✔	

(ii)

Quiscora Ltd will no longer be able to reclaim VAT on its purchases	
Quiscora Ltd will be issued with a notice of assessment	
Quiscora Ltd will be required to pay a penalty	✔

(c) **(i)** TRUE. To be eligible for the flat rate scheme a business must have an annual taxable turnover of less that £150,000. The exempt supplies are not taxable so Quiscora Ltd is eligible.

(ii)

0.5%	
1%	✔
10%	

(iii)

Cash accounting scheme	
Annual accounting scheme	✔

Task 7

(a)

Definition	Options
The system for calculating and applying deductions for Income Tax	Pay As You Earn (PAYE)
The amount of untaxed, or free, pay that an employee is entitled to in one year	Personal allowance
Amounts paid to the Government by employers and employees to fund benefits for people who are retired, sick or unemployed	National Insurance Contributions
The online process for submitting payroll information to HMRC	Real Time Information (RTI)

(b) (i)

	True	False
National Insurance Contributions are only made by employees		✔
Student loan repayments are a statutory payroll deduction that is made once an employee's earnings exceed a defined threshold	✔	
Union membership fees are a statutory deduction		✔
An employer is required to offer employees over the age of 22 a workplace pension, and must make contributions if the employee earns above a specified amount	✔	

(ii)

Form	Required distribution date
P60	31 May 2024
P11D	6 July 2024

(iii)

Form	Options
The form that an employee will have received from their previous employee, summarising information about their employment and pay to date	P45
The form that is submitted to HMRC detailing payments to employees, deductions made, and details of new employees and employees that leave	FPS

Task 8

(a) **(i)**

The warehouse supervisor	
Stella	✔
Francis	
The external accountant	

(ii) FALSE. The external accountant will need the monthly payroll analysis to complete the year-end accounts.

(iii)

The amount due to HMRC is ……	£5,897.10
The date this amount must be paid to HMRC by is …..	22 March 2024

(b)

The local college	
The gov.uk website	✔
Stella, the owner of the business	
Update from the payroll software provider used by Inkpen Ltd	✔
An article in a national newspaper	

(c)

The maximum reduction in Class 1 NIC an employer can get if it is eligible for employment allowance is £5,000	✔
Any business that claims employment allowance only needs to make quarterly payroll payments to HMRC	
A business may be eligible for employment allowance if its National Insurance Contributions do not exceed £100,000	✔
Employment allowance should be claimed on the employer's Full Payment Submission (FPS)	

Answers to practice assessment 3

Task 1

(a)

… that has been trading for more than three years	
… that makes at least some taxable supplies	✔
… with taxable turnover greater than the VAT registration threshold	

(b)

The business is not yet required to register as its taxable turnover for the past 12 months is below the VAT registration threshold	
The business must register without delay because the new order plus the average month's sales is for an amount in excess of the VAT registration threshold	✔
The business will exceed the VAT registration threshold in the 12 month period to 31 August and must register on 31 August	

(c)   **(i)**

Month	Standard rate supplies £	Zero rate supplies £	Monthly taxable supplies £	Cumulative taxable supplies £
May 2023	17,700	7,450	25,150	25,150
June 2023	18,900	6,900	25,800	50,950
July 2023	16,200	9,700	25,900	76,850
August 2023	17,200	5,400	22,600	99,450
September 2023	17,750	3,100	20,850	120,300

(ii)   31 August 2023

(iii)   30 September 2023

(d)

The cash accounting scheme	✔
The annual accounting scheme	
The flat rate scheme	

(e)

5%	
14.5%	
16.5%	✔
20%	

Task 2

(a) **(i)**

Vanessa will have to arrange payment to HMRC of £14,346	
Vanessa will have to reclaim £14,346 from HMRC	✔
Vanessa will have to arrange payment to HMRC of £35,380	
Vanessa will have to reclaim £49,726 from HMRC	

(ii)

Bromsing Ltd can issue a simplified invoice for standard-rated items of £215 plus VAT	
Bromsing Ltd can issue a simplified invoice for a mixed supply of zero-rated items of £80 and standard-rated items of £150 plus VAT	
Bromsing Ltd can issue a simplified invoice for a mixed supply of standard-rated items of £140 including VAT and zero-rated items of £100	✔

(iii)

The tax point	
The seller's VAT registration number	
The seller's address	
The amount of VAT	✔
A description of the goods and services	

(b)

1 May	
15 May	
21 May	✔
31 May	

(c)

£245.99	
£178.60	
£173.24	✔
£75.00	

(d)   £137.74

(e)

Net £	VAT £	Gross £
247.20	49.44	296.64
284.35	56.87	341.22

Task 3

(a)

VAT incurred on costs and expenses that have been paid for before the due date in order to obtain prompt payment discount	
VAT incurred on costs and expenses that have not been paid for at the end of the VAT accounting period	
VAT incurred on costs and expenses that cannot definitely be attributed to taxable supplies or to exempt supplies	✔
VAT incurred on costs and expenses that can definitely be attributed to taxable supplies or to zero-rated supplies	

(b)

	True	False
A business with average total input tax per month of £1,500, including exempt input tax of £600, can claim back all its input VAT	✔	
A business can claim back all input VAT if its exempt input tax is 20%, or less, of its total input tax		✔

(c) **(i)**

	Input tax recoverable	Input tax partly recoverable	Input tax blocked
The cost of the tickets for staff to attend an awards ceremony where Alkadi Ltd won an award	✔		
A business dinner with three members of staff from a prospective customer, attended by the sales manager and two of the sales team			✔
Centre court tickets at Wimbledon for a customer as a thank you for its business			✔

(ii) £720

Working: £4,800 x 20% = £960 x 75% = £720

(d)

Bad debt	Eligible for bad debt relief	Not eligible for bad debt relief	Amount of bad debt relief available £
Charles and Co was invoiced on 1 June 2023 for £2,340. It paid £1,422, but is disputing the remainder. The balance has been written off in the accounts of Alkadi Ltd	✔		153.00
Manuka Ltd owes a total of £2,745. Alkadi Ltd has not traded with Manuka Ltd for 12 months, and has set up a bad debt provision for 80% of the outstanding amount		✔	0.00

(e)

£270.33	
£134.00	
£70.50	
£67.50	✔

Task 4

(a)

Transaction	Change to input tax £	Change to output tax £
10 January 2023 £324, direct debit payment for the business's quarterly internet and telephone supply, on which standard rate VAT has been charged	54.00	0.00
24 January 2023 £3,360, cash from the sale of a business van. Homilies Ltd claimed input VAT on the original purchase of the van	0.00	560.00
12 February 2023 £4,123.98 paid to HMRC for VAT for the quarter ended 31 December 2020	0.00	0.00
1 March 2023 £196.35, payment from a customer for goods on which Homilies Ltd charges reduced rate VAT	0.00	9.35

(b)

	True	False
VAT on imports to the UK is normally charged at the same rate as if it had been supplied in the UK	✔	
If a VAT-registered business is using postponed VAT accounting, this means the payment of VAT is speeded up		✔
VAT on imports accounted for through postponed VAT accounting is included in the Box 1 and Box 4 figures on the VAT Return	✔	

(c)

The business makes standard-rated supplies and purchases zero-rated goods and services	
The business makes exempt supplies and purchases standard-rated goods and services	
The business makes zero-rated supplies and purchases standard-rated goods and services	✔
The business makes exempt supplies and purchases zero-rated goods and services	

Task 5

(a)   (i)   £32,762.74

       (ii)   £58,368.30

       (iii) - £25,605.56

(b)   (i)   Error 1 has resulted in **input** tax being **overstated.**

              Error 2 has resulted in **input** tax being **overstated.**

       (ii)   £195

       (iii)

Add £195 to Box 1	✔
Add £47 to Box 1	
Deduct £195 from Box 4	
Deduct £47 from Box 4	

(c)

£20,146	
£10,000	✔
£2,014.60	
£201.46	

(d)

Do not tell anyone and hope that the error is not discovered	
Correct the error on the next VAT Return despite knowing that it should be separately disclosed	
Explain to the Finance Manager that he has made the error and that the business must make a voluntary disclosure of the error	✔
Contact HMRC himself, and make a voluntary disclosure of the error	

Task 6

(a) **(i)**

	True	False
A default penalty of £200 is charged by HMRC if a business decides to deregister for VAT		✔
If a business fails to submit a VAT Return on time, HMRC can issue a VAT notice of assessment that estimates the amount of VAT due	✔	
Any late submission penalty points a business has automatically expire after a year		✔
HMRC cannot charge interest if a business does not report and pay the correct amount of VAT		✔

(ii) The rate of interest that HMRC can charge on VAT that is late is calculated as the Bank of England base rate plus 2.5%.

(b) **(i)**

January, May, September	
February, May, August	
March, July, November	
April, July, October	✔

(ii) £43,575

Working: £174,300/4 = £43,575

(iii)

31 December 2023	
31 January 2024	
10 February 2024	
28 February 2024	✔

(c)

	True	False
If VAT is due to HMRC, it will collect three days after the date that the VAT Return is due	✔	
If a repayment of VAT is due to a business, HMRC will make the payment three days after the date on which the VAT Return is due		✔

Task 7

(a)

Information	P60	P11D	Payslip
The amount of tax an employee has paid on their earnings in the tax year	✔		
The gross amount of pay in a pay period before any deductions			✔
Details of a company car provided to an employee		✔	
Private medical insurance paid for by an employer for an employee		✔	
The number of hours worked by an employee on a variable hours contract			✔

(b)

	£
Amounts received	20,697.43
PAYE	3,090.10
Employee's National Insurance Contributions	2,156.67
Amount per P60 in 2021/22	25,944.20

(c) **(i)**

£100	
£200	
£300	✔
£500	

(ii) An employer must keep payroll records for a minimum of **3** years after the end of the tax year to which they relate. Failure to do so may result in a penalty of **£3,000**.

Task 8

(a)

As the VAT rate is decreasing the business must consider whether the menu prices charged to customers, which are inclusive of VAT, should change. These prices **can remain unchanged if the business chooses.**
The new rate of VAT must be reflected in the amount of VAT we pay to HMRC **whether we change the prices to customers or not.**
If the date of the change in VAT rate falls during one of our VAT periods, our system must **apply both the old and the new rates of VAT during that VAT period, depending on the date of each meal.**

(b)

You have received an email from the software provider saying the software licence needs to be renewed	
One of the restaurant managers suggested that all computer software needs to be updated every two months	
You receive an email from HMRC about a change in the way in which VAT Returns are submitted	✔
When you log on to the accounting software there is a notification stating that an update is required	✔

(c) **(i)**

Ensure that the license for the accounting software is renewed annually	
Attending relevant Continuing Professional Development provided by AAT	✔
Having quarterly meetings with the owner of the busines to explain the content of the VAT Return	
Subscribe to the HMRC email updates on VAT and ensure you read them regularly	✔

(ii)

Integrity	
Confidentiality	
Professional competence and due care	✔
Professional behaviour	

Reference Material

For AAT Assessment of Tax Processes for Business

Finance Act 2023

For assessments from 29 January 2024

Note: This reference material is accessible by candidates during their live computer based assessment for Business Tax.

This material was current at the time this book was published, but may be subject to change. Readers are advised to check the AAT website or Osborne Books website for any updates.

Reference material for AAT assessment of Tax Processes for Businesses

Introduction

This document comprises data that you may need to consult during your Tax Processes for Businesses computer-based assessment.

The material can be consulted during the practice and live assessments by using the reference materials section at each task position. It's made available here so you can familiarise yourself with the content before the assessment.

Do not take a print of this document into the exam room with you*.

This document may be changed to reflect periodical updates in the computer-based assessment, so please check you have the most recent version while studying. This version is based on Finance Act 2023 and is for use in AAT Q2022 assessments in 2024.

*Unless you need a printed version as part of reasonable adjustments for particular needs, in which case you must discuss this with your tutor at least six weeks before the assessment date.

Note that page numbers refer to those in the original AAT Guidance document

Contents

1. Rates of VAT

Taxable supplies:

Standard rate	20%
Reduced rate	5%
Zero rate	0%

Non-taxable supplies have no VAT applied:

- Exempt
- Outside the scope of VAT

2. Registration and deregistration for VAT

Registration threshold	£85,000
Deregistration threshold	£83,000

Compulsory registration	Notify HMRC	Registration effective from
Historic test	Within 30 days of the end of the month threshold was exceeded	First day of the second month after threshold exceeded
Future test	Before the end of the 30 day period	From the start of the 30 day period

Deregistration	Notify HMRC	Deregistration effective from
Compulsory	Within 30 days of the business ceasing to make taxable supplies	Date of cessation
Voluntary	Evidence that taxable supplies will not exceed the VAT deregistration threshold in the next 12 months	Date request received by HMRC, or Agreed later date

3. Failure to register for VAT

- This can result in a penalty for failure to notify. The penalty is a % of potential lost revenue (PLR).

Type of behaviour	Within 12 months of tax being due		12 months or more after tax was due	
	unprompted	prompted	unprompted	prompted
Non-deliberate	0-30%	10-30%	10-30%	20-30%
Deliberate	20-70%	35-70%	20-70%	35-70%
Deliberate and concealed	30-100%	50-100%	30-100%	50-100%

- Penalties will not be applied if there is a reasonable excuse.

- HMRC will treat the business as though it had registered on time and will expect VAT to be accounted for as if it had been charged. The business has two choices:

    i. treat the invoices as VAT inclusive and absorb the VAT which should have been charged, or

    ii. account for VAT as an addition to the charges already invoiced and attempt to recover this VAT from its customers.

4. Changes to the VAT registration

HMRC must be notified of a change of:

Name, trading name or address	Within 30 days
Partnership members	Within 30 days
Agent's details	Within 30 days
Bank account details	14 days in advance
Change in business activity	Within 30 days

5. Keeping business and VAT records

Record retention period	6 years
Penalty for failure to keep records	£500

6. Contents of a VAT invoice

Full VAT invoice

- a sequential number based on one or more series which uniquely identifies the document
- the time of the supply (tax point)
- the date of issue of the document (where different to the time of supply)
- supplier's name, address, and VAT registration number
- customer's name and address
- a description sufficient to identify the goods or services supplied
- for each description, the quantity of the goods or the extent of the services, the rate of VAT, and the amount payable excluding VAT — this can be expressed in any currency
- the gross total amount payable, excluding VAT — this can be expressed in any currency
- the rate of any cash discount offered
- the total amount of VAT chargeable — this must be expressed in sterling
- the unit price (applicable to countable elements).

Simplified VAT invoices (<£250)

- suppliers name, address, and VAT registration number
- the time of supply (tax point)
- a description which identifies the goods or services supplied
- for each applicable VAT rate, the total amount payable, including VAT, and the VAT rate.

Modified VAT invoices

- a full VAT invoice showing the VAT inclusive rather than VAT exclusive values.

7. Partial exemption for VAT

De minimis amount	£625 per month
Proportion of total input VAT	<50%

- Generally, a partially exempt business cannot reclaim the input tax paid on purchases that relate to exempt supplies.

- If the amount of input tax incurred relating to exempt supplies is below a minimum de minimis amount, input tax can be reclaimed in full.

- If the amount of input tax incurred relating to exempt supplies is above the de minimis amount, only the part of the input tax that related to non-exempt supplies can be reclaimed.

8.   International trade and VAT

Export of goods	Zero-rated
Import of goods	UK VAT applied using postponed accounting.
Export of services	Apply UK VAT if place of supply is in the UK: • for supplies to business, place of supply is the location of the customer (outside the scope of UK VAT) • for supplies to non-business customers, place of supply is the location of the supplier (charge UK VAT).
Import of services	Reverse charge applies

9.   Tax points for VAT

Basic tax point date	Date of despatch of the goods/carrying out of the service
Actual tax point date may be earlier	If either: • payment is received earlier • invoice is issued earlier. Actual tax point becomes the earlier of these two dates.
Actual tax point date may be later	If: • invoice is issued within 14 days of despatch/service (and advance payment didn't apply).

- Deposits are treated separately to final payment and so may have a different tax point.
- The tax point is always the date of payment if cash basis is being applied.
- Where services are being supplied on a continuous basis over a period in excess of a month but invoices are being issued regularly throughout the period, a tax point is created every time an invoice is issued or a payment is made, whichever happens first.
- Goods on sale or return will have a tax point date either on adoption (the customer indicates they will keep the goods) or 12 months after removal of the goods where this is earlier.

10.   Time limits for issuing a VAT invoice

Within 30 days of tax point which is either:

- within 30 days of date of supply or
- within 30 days of payment if payment was in advance.

11. Blocked expenses and VAT

Input VAT cannot be recovered on blocked expenses.

Business entertainment

● The exception is that input tax can be reclaimed in respect of entertaining overseas customers, but not UK or Isle of Man customers.

● When the entertainment is in respect of a mixed group of both employees and non-employees (e.g. customers and/or suppliers), the business can only reclaim VAT on the proportion of the expenses that is for employees and on the proportion for overseas customers.

Cars

● Input VAT can only be recovered on cars if it is wholly for business (no private use).

● 50% of input VAT can be recovered when cars are hired/leased.

● VAT can be recovered on commercial vehicles such as vans/lorries.

Assets with private use

● The VAT recovery should be based only on the proportion related to business use.

12. Fuel scale charge and VAT

If the business pays for road fuel, it can deal with the VAT charged on the fuel in one of four ways:

● reclaim all of the VAT. All of the fuel must be used only for business purposes

● reclaim all of the VAT and pay the appropriate fuel scale charge (as follows) - this is a way of accounting for output tax on fuel that the business buys but that is then used for private motoring

● reclaim only the VAT that relates to fuel used for business mileage. Detailed records of business and private mileage must be kept

● do not reclaim any VAT. This can be a useful option if mileage is low and also if fuel is used for both business and private motoring. If the business chooses this option it must apply it to all vehicles, including commercial vehicles.

The fuel scale charge is as follows:

Description of vehicle: vehicle's CO2 emissions figure	VAT inclusive consideration for a 12 month prescribed accounting period (£)	VAT inclusive consideration for a 3 month prescribed accounting period (£)	VAT inclusive consideration for a 1 month prescribed accounting period (£)
120 or less	737	183	61
125	1,103	276	91
130	1,179	293	97
135	1,250	312	103
140	1,327	331	110
145	1,398	349	115
150	1,474	368	122
155	1,545	386	128
160	1,622	405	134
165	1,693	423	140
170	1,769	441	146
175	1,840	459	152
180	1,917	478	159
185	1,988	497	164
190	2,064	515	171
195	2,135	534	178
200	2,212	552	183

Description of vehicle: vehicle's CO2 emissions figure	VAT inclusive consideration for a 12 month prescribed accounting period (£)	VAT inclusive consideration for a 3 month prescribed accounting period (£)	VAT inclusive consideration for a 1 month prescribed accounting period (£)
205	2,283	571	190
210	2,359	588	195
215	2,430	607	202
220	2,507	626	208
225 or more	2,578	644	214

- Where the CO_2 emission figure is not a multiple of 5, the figure is rounded down to the next multiple of 5 to determine the level of the charge.

13. Bad debt and VAT

VAT that has been paid to HMRC and which has not been received from the customer can be reclaimed as bad debt relief. The conditions are that:

    i.   the debt is more than six months and less than four years and six months old

    ii.   the debt has been written off in the VAT account and transferred to a separate bad debt account

    iii.   the debt has not been sold or handed to a factoring company

    iv.   the business did not charge more than the normal selling price for the items.

Bad debt relief does not apply when the cash accounting scheme is used because the VAT is not paid to HMRC until after the customer has paid it to the supplier.

14. Due dates for submitting the VAT return and paying electronically

Deadline for submitting return and paying VAT – quarterly accounting	1 month and 7 days after the end of the VAT period
Deadline if being paid by direct debit	HMRC will collect 3 working days after the submission deadline.

- Please see alternative submission and payment deadlines for special accounting schemes.

15. Special accounting schemes for VAT

15.1 Annual accounting scheme for VAT

Joining the scheme	Maximum (estimated) taxable turnover in next 12 months	£1.35m	
Leaving the scheme	Compulsory if taxable turnover at the end of the VAT accounting year exceeds the threshold	£1.6m	
VAT returns	One annual return	2 months after the end of the accounting period	
VAT payments (monthly)	Nine monthly interim payments (10% of estimated VAT bill based on previous returns)	At the end of months 4 to 12 in the accounting period	
	Balancing payment	2 months after the end of the accounting period	
VAT payments (quarterly)	Three interim payments (25% of estimated VAT bill based on previous returns)	At the end of months 4, 7 and 10 in the accounting period	
	Balancing payment	2 months after the end of the accounting period	

15.2 Cash accounting scheme for VAT

Joining the scheme	Maximum (estimated) taxable turnover in next 12 months	£1.35m
Leaving the scheme	Compulsory if taxable turnover at the end of the VAT accounting year exceeds the threshold	£1.6m

15.3 Flat Rate Scheme for VAT

Joining the scheme	Taxable turnover (excluding VAT) in the next 12 months	£150,000
Leaving the scheme	On the anniversary of joining, turnover in the last 12 months (including VAT) or expected turnover in next 12 months	£230,000
Discount	In first year of being VAT-registered	1%
Limited cost business	Goods cost less than either: • 2% of turnover, or • £1,000 a year	16.5%
Capital expenditure	Input tax can be recovered on individual large capital purchases	£2,000

- The appropriate flat rate % will be provided in the assessment.

16. Errors in previous VAT returns

Adjustments can be made to correct errors that are:

- below the reporting threshold
- not deliberate
- for an accounting period that ended less than 4 years ago.

The reporting threshold is;

- £10,000 or less or
- up to 1% (maximum £50,000) of total value of sales and all other outputs excluding any VAT
- When the next VAT return is submitted, the net value is added to VAT due on sales and other outputs for tax due to HMRC, or to VAT reclaimed in the period on purchases and other inputs for tax due to you.

If the value of the net VAT error discovered is above the reporting threshold, it must be declared to HMRC separately, in writing.

17.   Late submission and late payment of VAT

17.1   Late submission

Submission frequency	Penalty point threshold	Period of compliance
Annual	2 points	24 months
Quarterly	4 points	12 months

Initial penalty	£200
Subsequent penalty	£200

Removal of penalty points

Business has not reached penalty threshold	Each point automatically expires two years from the first day of the month after the month when the late submission occurred.
Business has reached penalty threshold	All points will be reset to zero if both conditions below are met: • a period of compliance (meeting all submission obligations on time for the period of compliance), and • all submissions due in the preceding 24 months have been made (whether or not they were on time).

17.2 Late payment

Number of days overdue	First late payment penalty	Second late payment penalty
up to 15	None	None
16 to 30	2% on the VAT outstanding at day 15 *	None
31 or more	2% on the VAT outstanding at day 15 AND 2% on the VAT outstanding at day 30	A daily rate based on 4% per annum charged every day from day 31 until paid in full

* HMRC have stated that the first late payment penalty which applies to the first 30 days will not be charged until after 31 December 2023.

17.3 Interest charged

Interest is calculated at the Bank of England base rate plus 2.5%.

The Bank of England base rate will be given in the assessment.

18. Assessment of VAT

If a VAT Return is not submitted on time, HMRC will issue a 'VAT notice of assessment of tax' which will state how much HMRC think is owed.

If HMRC issue an assessment that is too low, a penalty of up to 30% can be charged for not telling them it is incorrect within 30 days.

19. Penalties for inaccuracies in VAT return

A penalty can be charged as a percentage of the potential lost revenue (PLR):

Type of behaviour	Unprompted disclosure %	Prompted disclosure %
Careless	0-30	15-30
Deliberate	20-70	35-70
Deliberate and concealed	30-100	50-100

20. Payroll record retention

Retention period	3 years
Penalty for failure to maintain records	£3,000

21. Types of payroll submission

Full payment submission (FPS)

- File on or before employees pay day.
- Include payments to and deductions for all employees.

Employer payment summary (EPS)

- File if no employees were paid in the month.
- Send by the 19th of the following tax month.

22. Payroll deadlines

Registering for PAYE	You must register before the first payday. You cannot register more than 2 months before you start paying people
Month end date for PAYE	5th of each month
Payment date for monthly payroll	22nd of each month if paid electronically. 19th otherwise. If monthly amounts are <£1,500, quarterly payments can be made
Provide employees with P60	31st May
Filing deadline for Expenses & Benefits forms	6th July
PAYE and Class 1A NIC payment date	22nd July if paying electronically. 19th July otherwise
PAYE settlement agreement submission date	31st July
PAYE and Class 1B NIC payment date	22nd October if paying electronically. 19th October otherwise

23. Penalties for late submission of payroll filings

Penalties may apply if:
- the FPS was late
- the expected amount of FPSs was not filed
- an EPS was not filed.

Number of employees	Monthly penalty
1 to 9	£100
10 to 49	£200
50 to 249	£300
250 or more	£400

Penalties may not apply if:

- the FPS is late but all reported payments on the FPS are within three days of the employees' payday (unless there is regular lateness)
- a new employer is late but sends the first FPS within 30 days of paying an employee
- it is a business's first failure in the tax year to send a report on time.

24. Penalties for late payroll payment

Late payment of monthly/quarterly payments

- The first failure to pay in a tax year does not count as a default.
- Late payment penalties apply to late payments and payments of less than is due.

Number of defaults in a tax year	Penalty percentage applied to the amount that is late in the relevant tax month
1 to 3	1%
4 to 6	2%
7 to 9	3%
10 or more	4%

Additional penalties will apply if:

A monthly or quarterly amount remains outstanding after 6 months	5% of unpaid tax
A monthly or quarterly amount remains outstanding after 12 months	A further 5% of unpaid tax

These additional penalties apply even where only one payment in the tax year is late.

Late payments of amounts due annually or occasionally

30 days late	5%
6 months late	Additional 5%
12 months late	Additional 5%

25. Penalties for inaccuracies in payroll filings

A penalty can be charged as a percentage of the potential lost revenue (PLR):

Type of behaviour	Unprompted disclosure %	Prompted disclosure %
Careless	0-30	15-30
Deliberate	20-70	35-70
Deliberate and concealed	30-100	50-100

for your notes

for your notes

for your notes

for your notes

for your notes

for your notes

for your notes

for your notes

for your notes

for your notes

for your notes

for your notes

for your notes

for your notes

for your notes

for your notes

for your notes

for your notes

for your notes

for your notes